For mine and Taylor's
dear friends - Ann and Barrett
Jo Hardwick

Photo: Michael Dunlap

Contents

i	Foreward
iii	An Interview with Taylor Hardwick
1	Introduction
7	Residential Projects
45	Commercial Projects
67	Institutional Projects
95	Noteworthy Selections
109	Acknowledgements
111	Credits
112	Index

Hardwick
Years of Design

A compendium of buildings and creative projects designed by
Taylor Hardwick over the course of his career as a practicing architect

Taylor Hardwick and Jo Hardwick

Photo: Alexandre Georges

First Printing: May, 2014

Copyright © 2014 by Taylor Hardwick

Produced and published by Taylor Hardwick, AIA, Emeritus
All rights reserved. No portion of this book may be reproduced—mechanically, electronically, or by any other means including photocopying—without written permission from the publisher, except for brief passages that may be quoted for reviews.

Book design by Jill Applegate Design

ISBN: 978-0-615-97671-6

Foreword

TAYLOR HARDWICK IS A VISIONARY, WHOSE CREATIVE mind has produced a legacy of buildings that have enriched his adopted hometown of Jacksonville, Florida.

One of Hardwick's early influences was the great modernist architect Eero Saarinen, who said: "Architecture is an art, and its driving force comes from its art characteristics." Indeed, Hardwick is an artist who is an architect, and an architect who is an artist.

We must remember that architecture is the most public of all the arts. Our city's buildings are out there for everyone to see and enjoy, not hidden inside a museum or a gallery. We share them on a daily basis. When buildings are creative and beautiful, they uplift our community. They nourish our existence.

This book illuminates the career and creations of Taylor Hardwick. It is a splendid compendium of his work, and it underscores his place among Florida's outstanding architects. Such attention is not only well deserved, but it is necessary. Unfortunately many buildings designed by Hardwick, as well as other aspiring architects who started their careers right after World War II, have often gone under-appreciated and have even been demolished. Recently, however, the collective works of these so-called "Mid-Century Modern" architects are enjoying a new wave of recognition, both popularly and scholarly, for their inventive designs and bold concepts.

It is ironic that architecture is perhaps the most fragile of all of the arts. Buildings made of stone and steel, with foundations cemented to the earth, are less likely to survive than a poem or a painting or a symphony or a book. Far too often the whims of fashion can easily bring about the destruction of the most carefully designed architectural masterpiece.

Most would agree that the *magnum opus* of Hardwick's sixty-year career is the Haydon Burns Public Library. It is not only an icon of its era but is also an exemplary case study in this tension between creation and destruction. The library was built on the site of the old City Hall, which was designed by the great architect Henry John Klutho in 1901 and was revered for its classical design and beautiful copper dome. By 1960 it was considered old-fashioned and out of style, so it was demolished. Hardwick's ultra-modern Haydon Burns Library was built in its place, and the new library was celebrated as Jacksonville's latest architectural marvel and a totally integrated work of art, both inside and out.

Almost a half-century later, the library had outgrown Hardwick's building. The Haydon Burns Library closed and was replaced by a newer, "more modern" facility. Public taste had also changed, and many thought that this 1960s library building was old-fashioned and unattractive. Plans were underway to demolish it and replace it with a bland high-rise condominium. Luckily, preservationists interceded and saved this wonderful mid-century landmark, and in 2013 the Jessie Ball duPont Fund purchased the building with plans to preserve it and give it new life.

If Klutho's earlier City Hall had been saved, it would be one of our city's most prized landmarks, an icon of its time. This speaks loudly to the notion that it is often hard to judge the value of a work of art or a building when it is still relatively new. Similarly, Hardwick's library building and the entire body of his architectural work have not been properly recognized until recently. If there was ever any doubt about its artistic worth, the vivid tapestry of his creativity highlighted in this book will lay that doubt to rest.

I predict that 100 years from now, when architectural historians come to visit Jacksonville, they will seek out the Haydon Burns Library building as one of the three or four most significant downtown buildings. The art and architecture of Taylor Hardwick will stand the test of time.

— Dr. Wayne W. Wood, Hon. AIA
author of *Jacksonville's Architectural Heritage: Landmarks for the Future*

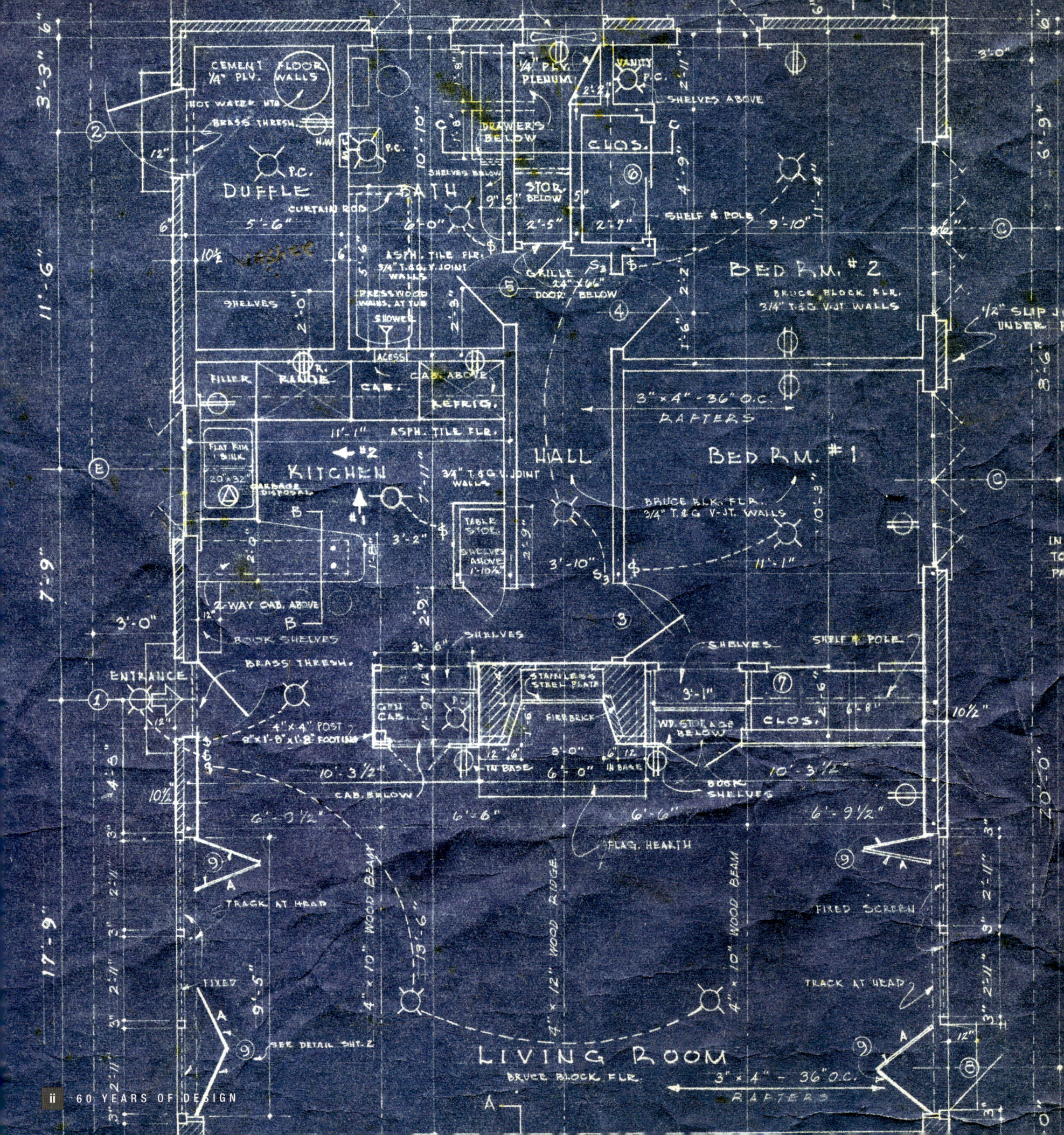

An Interview with Taylor Hardwick

Taylor Hardwick and Michael Dunlap, 2010

Left: Early construction drawing by Taylor Hardwick

AROUND 1968, MY STUDIES AT NATHAN Bedford Forrest High School landed me in a drafting class. These were the days of oversized, manila heavyweight paper and lead pencil holders. The pencils required a special black rotary sharpener, which indicated that I was in a rarefied environment.

As summer approached, I thought it would be a good idea to find a summer job. The school offered a clue in its cornerstone near the principal's office: The words "*Hardwick & Lee Architects*" were etched in stone. Since I had quickly become a school drafting legend, in my 16-year-old brain at least, working for these guys would be the thing to do.

With the assistance of my dear mom Betty Lou, I drafted a letter to the *Hardwick & Lee* office. I was sure to land a key spot on staff since I was backed up by my vast resume of 6 tattered drawings. Each sheet was graded with a small red letter "A" in the upper corner, and one with an "A+". I was destined for greatness.

It was a bubbly day at our house when a letter arrived from the *Hardwick & Lee* office. Taylor Hardwick actually responded to my request for summer employment, and he suggested a Saturday interview. I had no idea what an interview was, but a few elders assured me that I would be safe. It was mid-morning when the bus from deep Westside landed me near May Street, a few short blocks from the offices of Hardwick & Lee. I walked up a long flight of stairs to meet the architect. Mr. Hardwick was dressed casually in madras slacks and a polka-dot shirt, his style of dress clearly indicating that this man was not only an architect but also the "Coolest Guy on Earth!" The office was full of large flat tables, books, art, funny lights, and very large drawings of all sorts. This was the place where buildings were created; I was in way over my head.

The interview was underway. The confidence I had in myself and the fact that no pay seemed appropriate landed me my first real job. Mr. Hardwick, in his second act of kindness offered $20.00 per week, expressing his idea that "all work requires remuneration." I had to look up that word, too.

It was hard to fathom in 1968 what a sharp turn my life had taken, but now 30 years into my own practice, it can only be described as miraculous. All of the random events seemed to line up and set a course for my chosen profession, a course that was carefully steered by a very kind mentor, Taylor Hardwick. His kindness has lasted since those early days, days that were not easy. The multiple numbers of mistakes in the day-to-day work frequently resembled a sit-com. Taylor's edges were worn, but his patient skill, mentorship, and endless sense of humor carried us to the next day, the next week and far beyond. We both worked hard at my eventual evolution, through the subsequent summers and my long years at University of Florida. I was slowly becoming an architect, trained by a master as well as a University. This tutelage was priceless and great luck. His continuous support of my education and practice of architecture, which never seems to cease, is clearly a life treasure.

The friendship, now in its 45th year, is one of my life's true fortunes. As I write these words, it is my high honor to assist Taylor in the publication of this book. It is a book that celebrates and illustrates his profound talents as a Mid-Century architect, as well as his considerable skills as a writer, photographer, filmmaker, and community activist.

Jo Hardwick, whose tireless hours and love were given toward the book project, cannot escape mention. Her love for Taylor and the written word has made a great and well-received contribution to the project.

—Michael Dunlap

Photo: Michael Dunlap

Introduction

It was September of 1949 when Taylor Hardwick and his wife, Beezie (Louise Russell), decided to move to her hometown of Jacksonville, Florida. For two years, the couple had been living in a third floor walk-up apartment in downtown Philadelphia while Taylor attended graduate architectural school at the University of Pennsylvania.

Following his graduation in the spring of 1949, Taylor and Beezie reached the decision that urban living was not a choice for their next home. In addition, the job opportunities available at that time in the Philadelphia area were scarce or available only at large metropolitan firms. So, the Hardwicks packed up their 1948 Plymouth station wagon and headed south.

Taylor had visited Beezie's hometown of Jacksonville several times during their courtship and also during his 2½ years in aviation training with the US Navy. He had found the Florida coastal city ideal in size and climate. Jacksonville was growing rapidly in the post-war years, and the job opportunities were plentiful as well. They could stay at her parents' summer cottage in Atlantic Beach until settled into a home of their own.

After arriving in Jacksonville, Hardwick called on several local, small-firm architects whose practices were just beginning to thrive in the post-war environment. One of these was W. Kenyon Drake and Associates, a small firm of six. Drake and Associates was engaged in a variety of design projects at the time, and when Hardwick showed Mr. Drake his portfolio of graduate work and described some of his goals and ambitions, Mr. Drake listened attentively for five minutes, then said, "Yes. I can use you. When do you want to start?" It was the beginning of a learning experience that proved to be invaluable for the young architect.

As a neophyte, Hardwick was relieved to find that Mr. Drake's associates in the drafting room were willing to help him. His drawing board was central in line among five others, a location where his drawings were easily inspected by his cohorts. The more experienced architects and draftsmen became friends of Taylor as well as his mentors.

One of his early assignments was to produce a 3-dimensional, color rendering of a just-completed design: the First Christian Church of Jacksonville. It was an authentic Williamsburg brick colonial design with columns, steeple, and ornamental details—all well done, but completely beyond his college presentation experience, which was in contemporary modern design. Hardwick chose tempera as a medium and planned to use air brush for color and entourage. He struggled to adapt to traditional details and colors; his efforts, however, were in vain. The drawing he produced was, in his word, "terrible!"

Mr. Drake discerned his struggle and kindly told Hardwick not to worry. He then asked one of his talented partners to knock out a black and white aerial perspective drawing. While this first task felt like a failure for Hardwick, the defeat did not curb his enthusiasm nor cause him to abandon his determination to become a first-class architect. He was embarrassed but resolved to overcome his lack of skill.

Gradually, Hardwick became a valuable draftsman, working on a variety of projects. After a few months, Mr. Drake's close friend and client, Dr. Kenneth Morris, requested that Drake assign the design and construction drawings to Hardwick for a fishing lodge in Homosassa Springs, Florida. Mr. Drake graciously agreed and entrusted the project to his newest draftsman, who was surprised and delighted—his first real design challenge!

The lodge was to be for a weekend retreat, a one-story

continued on next page

Taylor Hardwick boarding his Stearman N2S Navy training plane in WWII.

Above photos, L to R: Homosassa Springs fishing lodge designed for Dr. Kenneth Morris in 1950; "Six Jaxons Pass Board of Architecture Exams," *Florida Times-Union* photograph, 1951, back row Taylor Hardwick, front row Mayberry Lee, License to Practice Architecture presenter Mellen C. Greeley, AIA, Secretary/Treasurer, Florida State Board of Architecture; Green Derby, location of *Hardwick & Lee, Architects'* first office. **Below:** Taylor Hardwick's logo, designed by Floyd Benton

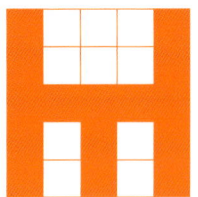

continued from previous page

cabin construction with kitchen, bunk-beds, and a roomy living area with comfortable furniture and a large fireplace. Plenty of storage space for cooking equipment as well as fishing gear was also included. The lodge was built on heavily wooded land on a lagoon. The cedar trees that grew on the property were cut to make room for the lodge and were used in the construction. The cedar boards were used for siding and framing lumber resulting in a beautiful and sturdy fishing lodge of simple, rustic design.

For the next two years, Hardwick became a comfortable, contributing member of the firm, learning and liking his chosen profession more and more. Gradually he gained the respect of his fellow workers for his creativity in design and his meticulously produced drawings.

In Florida, a prospective architect was required to work for a specified period of time as an intern for a registered, practicing architect in order to qualify as a candidate for the five-day written license examination. The exam covered the history of architecture, structural engineering, mechanical engineering, electrical engineering, ethics and procedures of business practices, and landscape design, plus an eight-hour design problem. The time with Mr. Drake had afforded Hardwick excellent preparation for all of these subjects. He completed the process successfully and received his State of Florida license in June of 1951. When told by Hardwick that he planned to leave employment in Kenyon Drake's firm and set up his own practice, Mr. Drake's response was, "Fine—I knew it all along. Good luck!"

With high expectations and gratitude for Mr. Drake's kind mentoring and best wishes, Hardwick ventured into the world of private practice. At first, he set up an office in the extra bedroom of his small subdivision home in suburban Lakeshore.

Several of the Hardwicks' friends and neighbors with growing families had spoken to Taylor about designing houses for them. He had responded, "As soon as I get my license." That was the beginning. At first, Hardwick undertook several remodeling projects; then clients for new houses called. He was soon forced to create a waiting list.

In the early months, Hardwick worked ten hours a day in his small office in the young couple's spare bedroom. The environment, however, was not conducive for creative conversations. Sometimes while clients were in conference with Taylor, Beezie was vacuuming the house, or their dog was barking at delivery trucks on the street. In addition, there was no air conditioning, and the attic fan was not much help. Papers from drawings were often sucked up and plastered against the fan's grill. Hardwick soon realized that he should find an office for his growing practice.

One day while talking to an architect friend, the topic of office locations came up. The friend mentioned that there was space for rent on the second floor above The Green Derby, a restaurant conveniently located on the corner of Riverside Avenue and Roselle Street in an area that was an office neighborhood on the outskirts of downtown Jacksonville.

Hardwick visited the building and was pleased to learn that it had been a retail store at one time with spacious offices on the second floor, accessed by a separate street entrance with stairs leading to a double-loaded corridor. Several offices and two restrooms, mostly used for dead storage, opened into the corridor.

The space for rent was a roomy, 20-foot square corner room near the stairs. It had large windows on two walls. The plaster walls and high ceiling as well as the oak flooring were

Above photos, L to R: May and Fisk Street office before remodeling; Atrium; Taylor Hardwick and Mayberry Lee, 1965

in good condition; the rent was surprisingly reasonable. During negotiations with the owner, however, Hardwick learned the necessary "sprucing up" of the office space, the corridor, the restrooms, the stairway, and street entrance was the responsibility of the tenant. It was a daunting task, but Hardwick was willing to undertake the challenge for the sake of his rapidly growing business.

Hardwick needed help in handling the accumulating commissions. His first thought was to contact Mayberry Lee, a young architect friend who had received his license at the same time as Hardwick. The two had engaged in many conversations on the nature of contemporary design and the future of the changing profession. They had also talked about helping each other as their respective careers developed.

Hardwick showed Mayberry The Green Derby office and offered him free rent there if he would help restore the premises and help in the catch-up of the lengthening client list of commissions. The two would split the fees equally. Lee agreed without hesitation to sharing space and business, and the cleaning began. In two weeks, Hardwick and Lee were established in the new, clean office with two large drawing boards and a new window air conditioner. Soon, the large office across the corridor was rented to Clayton Riley, who was a distributor of KIRBY vacuum cleaners. Every morning at 8:00 a.m., Riley met with his salesmen. During the meeting he gave a thirty-minute pep talk and led a singing session. Everybody on the second floor was soon pepped up and ready to go!

After several months of cooperative production, the two fledgling architects realized that they were a compatible duo who could have a successful career together. In 1952, Taylor Hardwick and Mayberry Lee formed the architectural firm of *Hardwick & Lee Architects, AIA*.

By 1955, the practice had outgrown The Green Derby office, and Hardwick began searching the Riverside area for a larger space for offices and parking. He located a vacant 1909 two-story frame cottage in a quiet residential area on the corner of May and Fisk Streets. The house was in good condition and could be easily remodeled.

The partners stripped down the second floor for a large drafting room and several offices. The first floor was converted to a large studio with comfortable living area. Hardwick rented the first-floor space to a graphic designer-advertising artist, John Ropp, who lived and worked there for 22 years until the building was sold to a developer.

Hardwick & Lee, Architects flourished in the cottage for three years before expansion was required. The neighboring house was an exact duplicate of the *Hardwick & Lee* house and was aligned only twenty feet to one side. After convincing the next-door neighbor to sell his house, Hardwick designed two enclosed, second-floor bridges between the two houses. The bridges provided ample expansion for *Hardwick & Lee*.

From 1959 until 1970, Hardwick had a contemporary furniture showroom located on the first floor of the second building. The showroom, Atrium, afforded his clients access to fine contemporary furniture that could not be found elsewhere in the Jacksonville area.

In 1962, Jacqueline Holmes and Taylor Hardwick formed a partnership and opened a contemporary art gallery, The Group Gallery, adjoining the furniture showroom and architects' offices. It was the first such gallery opened in Jacksonville.

During his 60-year career, Hardwick designed more than 150 custom houses, five high schools, five elementary

continued on next page

The architect should not be afraid to

continued from previous page

schools, and a classroom building at the University of Florida. He created dozens of commercial buildings, including the Fletcher Building, now known as the Florida Physicians Insurance Company. The variety of styles present in the work of *Hardwick & Lee* can often make it difficult to classify. In recent years the label "Mid-Century Modern" has been applied to the work of both Taylor Hardwick and Mayberry Lee and many of their prominent contemporaries. *Hardwick & Lee* used a variety of construction methods and visual motifs. Hardwick stated that he and his partner were always interested in innovating and consequently worked hard to avoid repeating themselves. Their work in the 1950s, primarily small residences and commercial buildings, included folded-plate roofs for long-span construction. Such roofs were not only economical but also attractive. The use of commercial building materials offered new possibilities for residential construction while color was an essential element in their designs.

In 1965 the firm completed its two largest and most important public commissions: the 14-acre Friendship Park and Fountain and the Haydon Burns Library, both in Jacksonville.

Strong lines and vaulting angles still occurred in Hardwick's solo work in the 1970s and 1980s. More subdued color and natural wood surfaces replaced the vibrant colors of the previous decade. During this period Hardwick developed design solutions for conquering the more challenging aspects of Florida terrain (swamps, rivers, abundant rainfall) with several structures built on stilts and others that were designed to float.

One of the two people most influential in Hardwick's work, was his partner Mayberry Lee. Both during his partnership with Lee and in the years following, Hardwick continued to acknowledge the vital contributions of his friend and partner in the success of the firm and to the personal success of Taylor Hardwick.

At the beginning of his career, Hardwick's one-hour meeting with the noted architect Eero Saarinen in 1949 was the most influential factor in the direction of his practice and his architectural designs. Saarinen counseled the young architect to establish his practice in a growing community that would be receptive to new ideas and to become an active member of the community he served.

Hardwick took Saarinen's advice seriously, and while he had become a member of the North Florida AIA upon receiving his license, in 1956 he was instrumental in establishing the Jacksonville Chapter of the AIA. He then served as the Jacksonville Chapter's president in 1959. He also served as a director of the Florida AIA at a later time as the representative of the Jacksonville Chapter.

Saarinen also offered four other memorable pieces of advice that Hardwick has not forgotten and, in fact, would himself offer to future architects.

First: An architect should not be concerned with style, neither to develop one's own style nor copy another's style. Each project deserves its own unique look.

Second: The architect should try to stay informed in the development of technology, new materials, and methods of construction that are coming out every year and rapidly changing the way buildings are constructed.

Third: The design should create a building that becomes a complementary part of the environment.

And his fourth piece of advice: The architect should not be afraid to experiment with new ways of design.

Hardwick used folded card-stock to experiment with roof angles and patterns.

4 60 YEARS OF DESIGN

experiment with new ways of design.

Residential Projects

The following pages depict a limited selection of residences designed by Taylor Hardwick and his firm, *Hardwick & Lee, Architects, AIA*, over a period of 60 years. Most of the houses displayed are located in Jacksonville, Florida, or its environs. The date of construction for each residence, and other buildings pictured in the book, may not be exact. Some dates may represent the start of construction while others may represent the end of construction. Some were built elsewhere, and their locations are noted. While Hardwick designed more than 150 homes during his years of practice, many residences of merit are not included in this book due to lack of space. Their exclusion is regretted. Nevertheless, the variety of homes found in the collection seen here represents the unique and versatile qualities of Hardwick's residential designs as well as his concern for simplicity and detail.

Hardwick believed that the relationship between the architect and the home-owner client is a stronger one than that experienced with a commercial or institutional group. The understanding of the goals and needs for the project could be determined through the interchange of ideas in face-to-face conferences and conversations better than through memoranda issued by corporate groups. The homeowner and architect worked closely as a team in planning and in execution. There were no surprises. The final product resulted in feelings of personal satisfaction, and for Hardwick, it was deeply rewarding to see families happy in the homes which he and they had created together.

Taylor Hardwick Residence

Bayview Residence Addition

1951 | Jacksonville, Florida

The Hardwicks bought their first home in 1949 and lived there until 1953. The house was located in an area of Lakeshore called "Splinterville" by the residents, a sobriquet derived from the use of tree names for the streets of the area.

The Hardwick house on Bayview Avenue, along with others in the area, had been built in 1941 as Navy housing. The design of the houses was uniform in construction and accommodation: three bedrooms, one bath, a tiny kitchen, a living/dining room, and screened porch.

All the houses had an under-floor heating system and an attic fan for cooling. The construction was wood frame with asbestos wall shingles and asphalt roofing shingles. Most had driveway ribbons, or narrow strips of concrete, and a one-car, separate garage.

A local real estate company had bought the entire subdivision and attracted young couples returning from military service with low selling prices and VA financing.

During the Hardwicks' time of residence on Bayview, the architect/owner added a wraparound screened porch with flagstone floor to the small frame house. The porch was a self-constructed project, the architect doing all the work himself.

In adding the porch, Hardwick built a new roof to cover the porch's entire length, thus effectively shrouding the living room windows in darkness. Therefore, he placed skylights in the porch roof over each window to provide light to the living room.

His job as a fledgeling architect allowed him only weekends and nights to master and apply all the construction techniques needed to accomplish his design. He learned new skills and a new respect for the artisan builders who create our living environment.

After many hours of hard work, Hardwick succeeded in the construction of a beautiful front screened porch that added an elegant touch to an otherwise ordinary frame house.

Top: Hardwick handcrafted the unique columns supporting the porch roof. **Left:** Because the new porch covered the living room windows, Hardwick placed large skylights over them. **Above:** The house before renovation showing the original screened porch.

RESIDENTIAL

Champ Taylor Residence
1952 | Jacksonville, Florida

In the early 50s, Dr. Champ Taylor, a young, practicing OB/GYN, was Taylor Hardwick's neighbor in "Splinterville," a community of World War II Navy-built homes in suburban Lakeshore.

Hardwick's house on Bayview Avenue was directly behind Champ Taylor's. The doctor was often "on call" and sometimes arrived home at very late hours. As he turned into his drive, Dr. Taylor's headlights would shine on the Hardwicks' windows, and if he saw any activity in the Hardwick house, he blinked his lights to signal an invitation to visit.

The two men engaged in many late-night discussions. During one of the discussions, Dr. Taylor described the house of his future and asked that Hardwick design it. Both expressed their intention to create a contemporary design and spent many hours in the formulation of what became the kind of house one might find in a forest.

The completed home was the first large, contemporary residence built in the design-controlled subdivision of Ortega Forest; therefore, approval for the modern, innovative design was obtained with much difficulty.

The design, however, fit comfortably in its environment surrounded by trees and shrubs, and both men were pleased with the result—a home of simple construction, without ornamentation. The house had generous interior spaces suited for the large family who lived there. An added benefit was the close friendship that developed between the two families during the design and construction period of the residence.

Dr. Taylor owned a farm in West Virginia near the Greenbrier Hotel. The doctor and his family often visited the farm where he felt close to his boyhood roots. Hardwick designed Dr. Taylor's home in Ortega Forrest to recall the farm buildings of the doctor's youth.

A few years after the construction of his Ortega Forest home, Dr. Taylor joined with another OB/GYN specialist, Frank McCall. That partnership prospered to the point of needing larger office space. Dr. Taylor located a property in the suburban area of Five Points, and he, McCall, and other physicians developed the property to become the 1661 Medical Building, which Taylor Hardwick designed. A description of the 1661 Medical Building can be found in the Commercial section.

Above: Street view of Taylor home.
Right: West elevation

Waldo Stockton Residence
1952 | Jacksonville Beach, Florida

This experimental two-story frame beach-rental house was built one block from the ocean. The owner told Hardwick that he wanted something different and preferably something less expensive than the existing cottages in the neighborhood.

Hardwick's design called for a newly developed construction technique—a modular framework of 4" x 4" pressure treated pine posts spaced 4 feet on center with 2½"-thick Cemesto sandwich-insulated panels and windows fitted between.

The Celotex Corporation developed Cemesto industrial panels in 1930. They were made by creating a rigid sandwich of ¼"-thick asbestos cement sheets with 2" of asbestos insulation glued between them. The panels were manufactured in a 4' x 8' size and could be sawn and fastened with machine tools. The panels were extremely strong, weatherproof, and had high thermal insulation ratings. The most common use was for roof panels, used here. The panels were used also as walls, however, in the Stockton residence.

Nicknamed "Flat Top," the building became an extremely popular and profitable rental property for many years. For several summers, the regular tenant was noted author Pat Frank, who became a good friend of Waldo Stockton.

The unpainted panels at "Flat Top" were still in their original condition when the building was demolished after 30 years of beach exposure.

Top: South and east exposures showing 4" x 4" pine posts forming modular framework. **Bottom:** Unpainted panels withstood beach elements for years.

10 RESIDENTIAL

Marion King Residence

1953 | Jacksonville, Florida

In 1953, the original owners of this house were a young couple who had started a new business manufacturing concrete blocks. New construction was booming after World War II, and a great demand for concrete blocks existed for both commercial and residential construction. Only one other local company, however, was making this material in the early 50s.

Marion King was a young man at the time, interested in new ideas. He spent much of his time introducing local architects to the variety of sizes and design qualities of his product and also the many uses it could serve.

King noted that residential developers used the concrete blocks mostly for foundations and exterior walls in low-cost housing. He wanted to demonstrate that his product could serve as the major material, both inside and out, if the residence was designed creatively. In order to prove his theory, King challenged *Hardwick & Lee Architects* to produce an aesthetic design for his own home, using the concrete blocks. The result, published in several design magazines, was an amazingly enduring home whose aesthetic qualities equaled its durability.

Marvel and Howie Wallace bought the home in 1955 and have lived there for nearly 60 years, maintaining the home in an almost like-new condition.

The site for King's innovative home was in Clifton, a tree-covered, undeveloped suburban area just east of the St. Johns River and not far from King's plant. Proving that a sleek, modern dwelling could fit compatibly within a heavily wooded site was the surprising result of the design and led many followers to do the same. Today the iconic example of residential Mid-Century architecture remains in much the same condition as 60 years ago.

Top: The red door of the front entrance echoes the red of the exposed steel bar joist that supports a lengthy, covered front walkway. **Right:** The light-filled living area displays the creative use of concrete blocks on the interior to form a partial separating wall.

RESIDENTIAL 11

George Varn Residence
1953 | Jacksonville, Florida

Top: Riverfront view from bluff. **Middle:** The stained wood siding gave a look of naturalness to the house nestled under the canopy of trees. **Bottom:** Hardwick designed the special cabinet wall as a pass-through to accommodate stereo and glassware/china storage.

The client was one of Hardwick's first residence commissions after he opened his practice. Aware of Hardwick's interest in contemporary architecture, the owners believed the young architect could carry out their ideas to custom design their new home.

It was the first house of modern post-war design to be built on a high riverfront bluff in Ortega. All rooms in the living area faced the St. Johns River, each with sliding glass doors, an innovative addition to home construction in the early 50s.

Located in an area with a large tree canopy, the house design included a riverside screened porch the length of the house so that the residents could enjoy the river while protected from insects. The construction of the high ceilings around the outside porches, along with the fiberglass screen and sliding doors, enabled the southeast breeze to circulate throughout the house.

The owners were interested in furniture design and cabinetry, and they requested a special pass-through cabinet wall to separate the kitchen and the dining room. Hardwick designed the cabinet to accommodate a stereo system with speakers and storage, integrating materials that complemented each other as well as the room.

The use of stained wood siding for all exterior walls gave the building the look of belonging in its natural environment—one of Hardwick's hallmarks in design.

RESIDENTIAL

The following is an article written by Taylor Hardwick in 1949 while he was an architecture student at University of Pennsylvania. It won the First Prize Samuel Huckle Award, in a University of Pennsylvania graduate essay competition.

A discussion of the desirability of simplicity in composition and how it may be generally achieved in architecture, and consequently, with what three phenomena of expression it is basically associated.

Simplicity is the utmost expression of truth and is obtained through complete solidity and few planes. The degree of expression of simplicity varies inversely with the number of limiting planes, openings or voids of a form and varies directly with volume magnitudes.

Simplicity indicates proper, logical restraint consistent with purpose, materials, size and the expression desired. Simplicity in composition requires the elimination of all irrelevant elements or details. Studied simplicity should not be confused with primitiveness, immaturity or lack of skill, for these are a result of inherent naivety.

Simplicity is the utmost expression of truth

Simplicity is primarily associated in our minds with speed of perception, speed of comprehension and significance. These factors make the achievement of simplicity in architectural compositions somewhat more difficult than in other forms of art expression. Yet the existence of these factors is a challenge to satisfy the need of humans to understand. A piece of sculpture is much more readily perceived and understood than a piece of architecture. The mind's desire to understand must be satisfied and the more quickly, the more simple an object must be.

Example: *The Florence Pitti Palace street façade. The details are designed to be perceived from a busy street by people hurrying by—the details are large, the rustication exaggerated. The Garden Front façade is designed to be perceived leisurely—it is less powerful—delicate detail—the scale is greater as the view from garden broadens.*

The instruments of simplicity are shape, mass, form, and silhouette; each of which is tremendously important.

Mass especially contributes to simplicity. The fewer planes involved in a form the more simple it is. The pyramids of Egypt have the greatest of simplicity in their dignity of form. The Gothic Cathedral is as great in mass as our largest skyscraper; yet it is far simpler than the skyscraper because it is one large void. The skyscraper is a collection of cells, a conception far inferior to either the pyramid or the cathedral.

Shapes control simplicity to a great extent, for areas enveloped by limiting lines are the most apparent description of simplicity; The Temple mounds of Yucatan, though a profusion of details, may be considered impressive when viewed from a distance, or seen in a silhouette.

The phenomenon of form can produce in architecture results most vital to the achievement of simplicity. Consideration for human elements and the ability to transform and transfigure materials are components. The treatment of planes and volumes to produce a building of significance must be dexterous and knowing.

Color can be used as a supplementary donor to heighten the sensual effect. The Alaskan Totem poles and Greek Temples exemplify the use of color in accord with form. Colors achieve, when used with understanding, an additional special balance and visual impression. They can extend boundaries and add space.

Simplicity can be achieved through a fundamental understanding of the nature and the implications of shapes, form and mass silhouettes. These elements can lead to simplicity, but cannot be considered as the only knowledge or philosophy necessary to produce an architectural composition with significant simplicity. A true insight is needed, that is, insight evolved painfully from knowledge and understanding. It is said that significant art comes from significant artists. The struggle, then, becomes one for honest self-knowledge and self-understanding, for an individual can become significant only by this means.

RESIDENTIAL

Taylor Hardwick Residence
1953 | Atlantic Beach, Florida

This home was the first oceanfront residence built in Atlantic Beach since the 1930s. Its contemporary design was celebrated in such publications as *Look Magazine*, which ran a three-page article on the unique design. The house was also featured on NBC's *The Morning Show with Dave Garroway*.

The "corn crib" shape is derived from Hardwick's childhood years living on a farm in Pennsylvania. Next to the barn behind his house was a corn crib of a design common to the region. It had a center aisle with storage on both sides for corn ears. The inside walls were vertical with gates; two exterior walls were sloped outward to increase air circulation without admitting rain. All walls were ½" hog wire. The stored corn was air dried over the winter from air flow through the building.

When Hardwick found an available 50-foot wide oceanfront building lot, very scarce and hard to find, in Atlantic Beach, Florida, he immediately thought of the corn crib of his boyhood home.

The prevailing southeast breeze could cool the house if he let it go through the building as the corn crib did with the corn.

The local building code required a 5-foot setback on each side, so he had only 40 feet for his building; however, the code allowed a 3-foot overhang for eaves.

Hardwick used this measurement for his roof overhang and connected the roof to the floor line creating enclosed storage and also rain protection for the windows. The shape proved that beach living for the Hardwick family could be as good as corn!

An unexpected thrill occurred in the first days of living there. The usual fleets of pelicans often seen traveling up and down the coast seemed to enjoy flying over the house and peering down through the skylight over the master bedroom.

In the living room a 7-foot-high wall of brick with large fireplace separated the master bedroom and bath from view. The high, rafter beams and cedar decking that formed the ceiling allowed air to flow through the house. Fire bricks were chosen for the wall for their size and color.

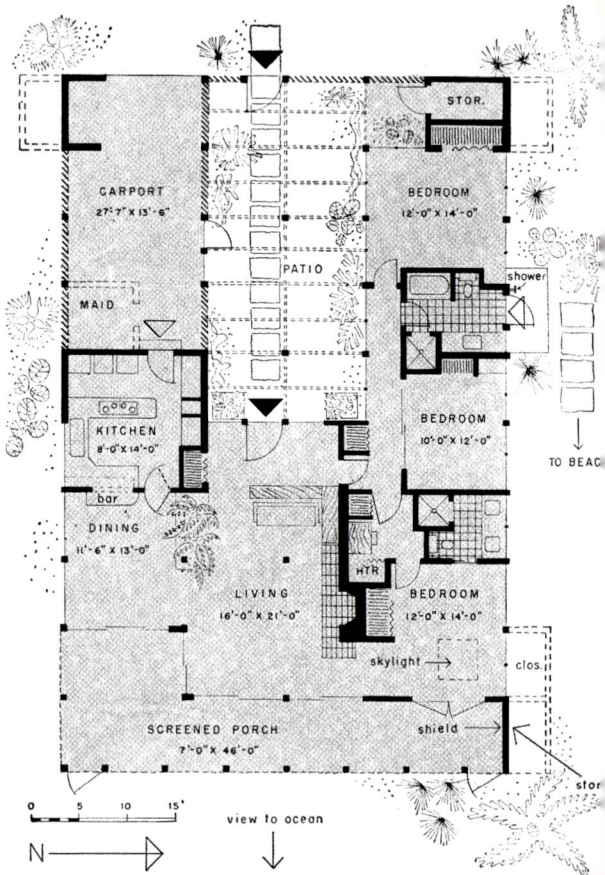

Top right: Hardwick's floor plan for his airy oceanfront house was inspired by the open-slatted corn crib from his childhood family farm. **Above:** Hardwick designed the patio to act as an air shaft in the middle of the plan, as an entrance court, as a sitting terrace, as a screened porch, and as a greenhouse. **Right:** A screened porch extends the length of the oceanfront elevation.

Left: Yellow-brown firebrick made up entire fireplace wall, with open space above to let breezes into bedroom at far left. Multi-colored stained-glass panes over sliding glass doors softened ocean glare. Durable, easily cleaned floor was terrazzo.

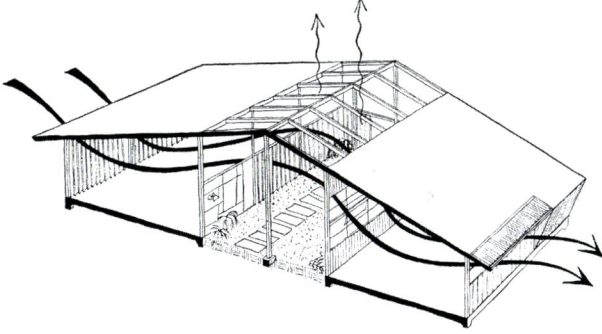

Top: (Bedroom) The bedroom skylight gave owners a view of stars—and flocks of shore birds—from their bed. On the north side of the roof, it got little direct sunlight. Glass doors opened to screened porch.
Above: (Diagram) Cross ventilation channeled breezes through entire building, an important feature since central air conditioning was not an option in 1953. **Above:** (Photo) Street elevation.

RESIDENTIAL 15

Thomas Peacock Residence
1953 | Jacksonville, Florida

The Florida Machine & Foundry Company had brought members of the Peacock family here from Scotland because of their several generations of expertise in steel foundry work.

And so it was that the Peacocks, father and sons, were especially appreciative of Hardwick's knowledge of building construction and also his well-founded suggestions when Thomas Peacock commissioned Hardwick to design his home.

The Empire Point subdivision was relatively new, and the client picked a choice riverfront lot overlooking a St. Johns River estuary. The river scene now includes a striking view of the Dames Point Bridge in the background, with the cable lights of the bridge adding a bonus of lighted beauty on a clear night.

Hardwick designed the house specifically for this steel foundry executive who approved the use of industrial materials to be exposed in the interior spaces. Sliding glass doors were installed in all the riverfront rooms. Steel bar joist, roof rafter beams were exposed for ceilings, with 3"-thick stained wood decking spanning them.

Exposed refractory bricks were used to make a 6-foot-high fireplace wall to separate the dining and living areas. The fireplace chimney vent was an exposed Cemesto pipe rising through the high ceiling.

Top: The two-sided fireplace was constructed with fire bricks; the raised hearth was topped with marble. **Left:** The dining room featured the other side of the fireplace wall. **Above:** Front entrance.

16 RESIDENTIAL

The exposed bar joist rafters extended the length of the ceiling on either side of the ridge beam. The ceiling was composed of cedar decking. Sliding glass doors opened to the riverfront terrace with the St. Johns River beyond. The north exposure of the living area allowed the architect to design a wall of glass, avoiding the intensity of the sun in either the morning or the afternoon.

O'Donoghue Residence

1956 | Jacksonville, Florida

The design was an early split-level house in the San Jose area utilizing new 5-foot-wide fiberglass insect screen on the 2-story living area. Sliding glass doors opened onto the screened areas.

Mr. O'Donoghue was a pioneer in the sale of architectural products in Jacksonville. Having established his business in the early 1950s, he was active in presenting new products to Jacksonville's practicing architects. He kept in touch with trends in design throughout the country and acquired unique franchises for the best new products.

Aluminum sliding glass doors were one of his exclusive lines. *Hardwick & Lee* was the first firm in Jacksonville to use Arcadia sliding doors manufactured in California and supplied by Jeff O'Donoghue.

Above: Interior view of zig-zag screened balcony and living area, which had ample space for tall tropical plants. **Left:** Architect's rendering showing two-story screened areas accessed from house via sliding glass doors.

Adair Springfield Residence

1958 | Jacksonville, Florida

A professional couple with the desire for an open-plan house, the Springfields chose a heavily wooded lot with a river view in the Clifton area suitable for the house's design requirements.

This distinguished two-bedroom house had a two-story high living and dining area. A narrow, carpeted stair led to a balcony overlooking the entire space below. The railing on the stair and balcony was of minimal design that allowed full view of the high walls that were almost completely covered by the Springfields' art collection of 50 years.

The framed paintings, drawings, and prints were placed closely together so that a potpourri of art could be seen from any vantage point. Fixed-glass gables of the exposed beam roof brought in the daylight to display this fine collection.

A flat diamond roof (a favorite Hardwick idiom) sheltered the double carport in front of the entrance to the house.

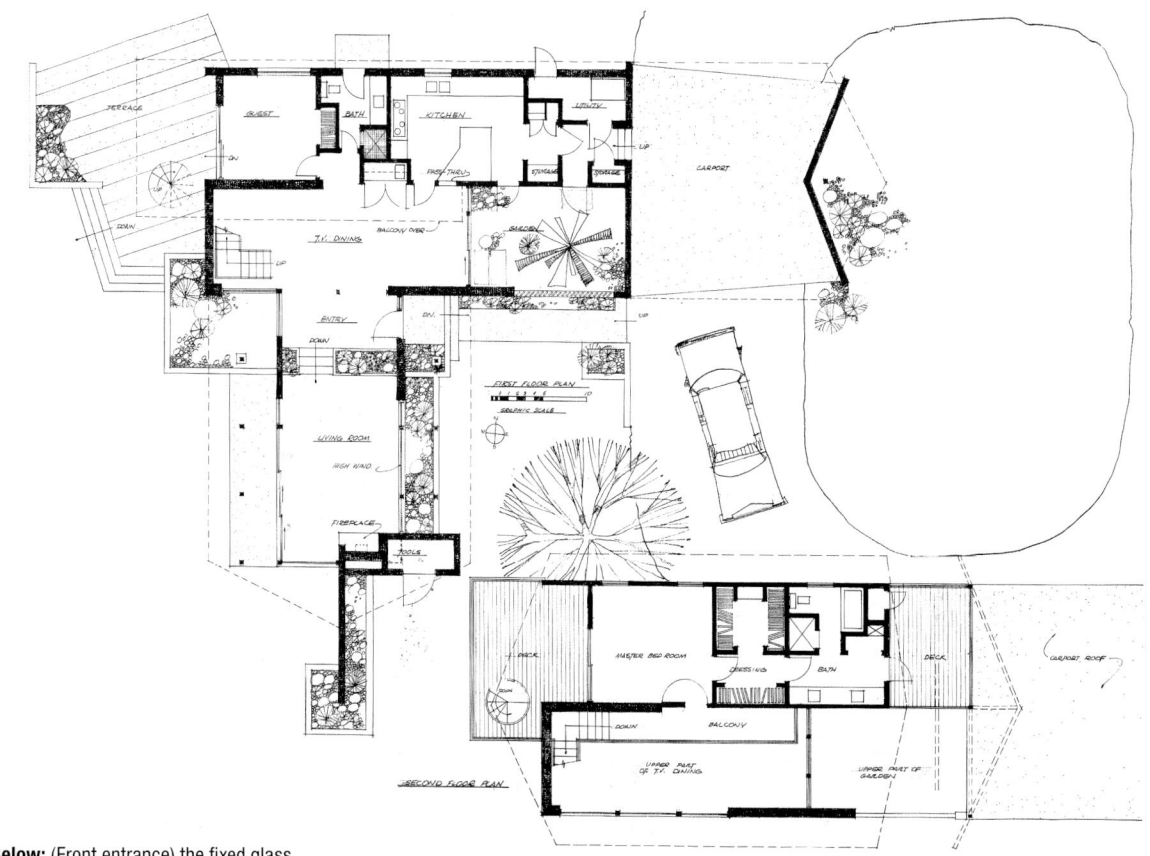

Below: (Front entrance) the fixed glass gables above the flat diamond carport roof reveal the exposed beam roof construction.

Robert Jacobs Residence

1962 | Seminole Beach, Florida

Robert Jacobs, a young bachelor executive chose for his residence a remote oceanfront site atop a high dune near Mayport. His needs were solitude, privacy, and a flow of space for entertainment.

As a member of the construction industry, the client was interested in experimental structural concepts and materials. To withstand the extreme, ocean-borne wind, Hardwick developed a roof system of flat-diamond-shaped, pressure-treated wood trusses on rows of columns. The trusses were roofed on top with plywood and shingles and finished on the bottom with 2′x 6′ cedar boards, spaced ⅜″ apart, forming the finished ceiling.

Air-conditioning ducts were installed throughout the enclosed attic, and cooled air was dispersed through the openings between the cedar boards. The design created an uninterrupted ceiling surface with neither air-conditioning vents nor lighting fixtures. Lighting was accomplished through fixed wall brackets.

Jacobs required a large swimming pool, and Hardwick designed an L-shaped pool as an integral part of the house plan. One could step from the living room right into the pool as though moving into another room. The pool had underwater speakers, an innovation for residential pools at that time. The surrounding terrace and pool contributed aesthetically to the design of the two-bedroom house.

Hardwick also designed a carefully detailed privacy wall as shelter from the road for the swimming pool and house. An electric-controlled gate kept vehicles from entering without approval.

The January 16, 1963, issue of *Town & Country* magazine featured a twenty-page article titled "A City in Transition." The article described the growth of Jacksonville and its future. Four pages of the story were devoted to the Robert Jacobs residence.

Above: South half of living area sheltered pool from Northeast wind. **Right:** The raised entrance led past the bath house wing to a front door that had electric controls. The entry was enhanced by a combination of white bricks and redwood bench.

Left: Terrace on ocean side was sheltered by 6-foot roof overhang bracketed by white brick walls and a fireplace. Side walls were green-stained redwood board and batten.

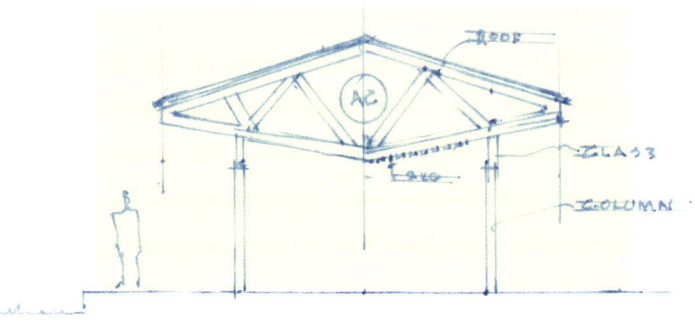

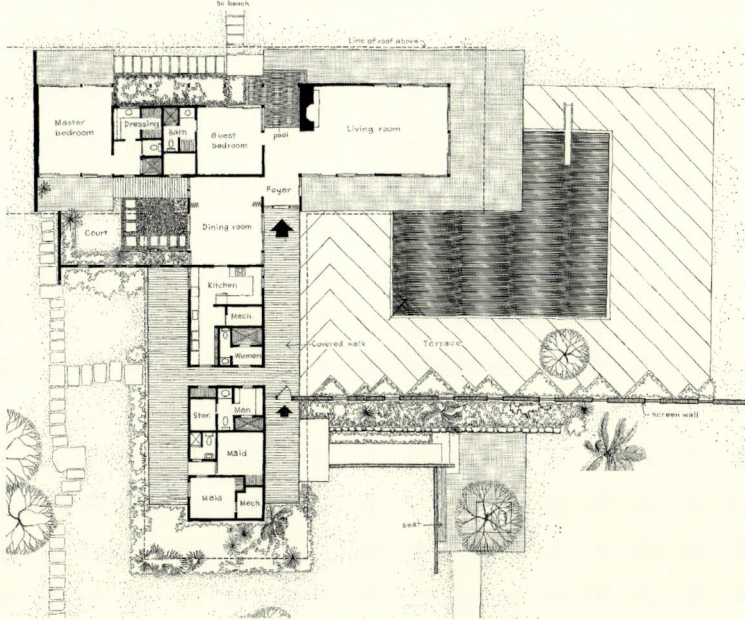

Above, left: Dining room and master bedroom opened to sheltered garden. **Above, right:** Louvered redwood panels between brick modules helped control wind movement and created privacy for bathers. **Left:** Architect's drawing of floor plan. **Far left:** Privacy wall shielded pool and house.

RESIDENTIAL 21

Whitehead Residence
1962 | Orange Park, Florida

The new owner of a late 1940s riverfront house requested Hardwick to remodel and expand the existing residence. Hardwick's design included the addition of a second floor with stair tower and a large entrance patio.

The patio was formed by walling off a portion of the walkway from the garage to the front door. Visitors were admitted by intercom through the patio to an ornamental front door.

Hardwick designed the patio, with its decorative paving, to serve as a sculpture gallery/garden. The exterior wall gave privacy to the area, thus creating a pleasant surprise to visitors as they entered the home.

Other alterations increased ceiling height in the living area where the grand piano was located. The resulting arrangement of the surfaces in the living room enclosure produced superior acoustics for music.

Windows in the living area were removed and replaced by a continuous wall of glass sliding doors, to take advantage of the impressive view of the St. Johns River and to open the house to the southeast breeze.

Top Left: Driveway entrance to patio shielded by privacy wall from garage to house. **Top Right:** front patio designed as sculpture gallery and garden. Decorative paving added interest to the flat surface. **Above:** The riverfront elevation showing the continuous wall of glass sliding doors that could be opened to admit cooling breezes or closed with no interference of the river view. **Left:** Stair tower with floating treads leading to the second floor addition.

Taylor Hardwick Residence
Addition and Remodeling
1964 | Jacksonville, Florida

Top: Enhanced circular driveway and remodeled street front showing new west wing and screened connection to existing house. Two-car zig-zag carport and laundry on left. **Left:** Original street front of the 1905 house with view of the St. Johns River in the background.

In 1960, Hardwick learned that a couple who owned a home in "Old Ortega" was considering selling the property. He visited the couple several times and made an offer to purchase the home, built in 1905. They accepted.

The house was a modest and austere two-story wood-frame, frugally built building with three bedrooms and two baths. It had small double-hung windows, no central heat nor air conditioning, and few closets. Nevertheless, it was a viable structure, and the beauty of the environment with its river view was outstanding.

To convert the box-like house into a nature-friendly family home, Hardwick decided not to remove any existing elements but to add complementary forms to new spaces.

The shape of the original house was a rectangular, two-story gabled box with a projecting gabled bedroom wing on one end, thus forming an L-shape. Following careful inspection of the premises and observation of the beautiful river view, Hardwick determined to add a two-story gallery wing, making the house aesthetically symmetrical. The riverfront of the new room was all glass from floor to pointed gable. To the north, was a spectacular view of the river and the City of Jacksonville, nine miles away.

The entire two-story wing that was added to the east side of the house matched the west wing of the existing building. He also lowered the new two-story wing's first floor four feet in order to gain greater wall height and maintain symmetry of roof. The rough-sawn wood walls were 28 feet high. A balcony was attached to and aligned with the second floor of the existing house, providing access from the second floor of the old house. The balcony could also be reached by a spiral stair leading from the newly created great room.

continued on next page

continued from previous page

The resulting wall space in the great room now provided space for the Hardwicks' extensive art collection. During his adult years, Hardwick had become a serious collector of modern art. His collection included many large paintings for which he had lacked sufficient wall space for display. He had long hoped to find or build a house with extremely high walls. Therefore, when this house on Ortega Point became available, he knew he could add what he needed.

The completed design received much publicity both locally and nationally in various publications. The August 1964 issue of *Ladies Home Journal* featured an eight-page photographic study of the house.

Clockwise from top: The high wall above the living room fireplace provided space for large paintings. The cast stone shelf served as a fireplace mantel and display place for sculptures. It then continues to the outside patio, topping the retaining wall. The retaining wall and interior wall on either side of the fireplace was constructed of granite ballast stones recovered from the shipping era; terrace steps led down to the riverfront lawn; riverfront elevation showing glass wall on wing addition and first and second floor exterior balconies on remodeled original wing; dining room with an antique chandelier recovered from an old house; twilight view of house as it appeared in *Ladies Home Journal*.

Photography by Alexander Georges. Author: Margaret White. Reprinted with permission from Meredith Corporation, ©2010 Meredith Corporation. All rights reserved.

The living room floor was dropped four feet to make the new roof match the existing roof. Above left a balcony overlooked the living area. Both sides of the room had a retaining wall of ballast stones topped by granite cast stone shelf.

RESIDENTIAL 25

Kafka Residence

1965 | Jacksonville, Florida

An ordinary 1930s brick house in the Venetia neighborhood achieved leisure space and identity by the addition of a full-length screened porch overlooking the Florida Yacht Club lagoon and the St. Johns River. The riverfront view of the home exemplified Hardwick's efforts to achieve simplicity and harmony in his designs as well as a rhythmic quality reminiscent of music.

"I call architecture frozen music," wrote Johann Wolfgang von Goethe in a letter to a friend in 1829. "When, as a student, I first read his words, I thought how much they fit my love for music," Hardwick observed. "The quality of music dominates both arts: music and architecture. In my own early designs, I had already unconsciously included visual rhythms. As I progressed in my creative efforts, the use of varied rhythms became a normal consideration pervading my designs. The Kafka residence is a simple example of the rhythm of 'frozen music,' and the Haydon Burns Library is a complex example of the ways rhythm has influenced my work."

26 RESIDENTIAL

Jennifer Johnson Gregg Residence
1967 | Jacksonville, Florida

Hardwick designed a one-story home in the Avondale area. It was built on pilings on a river-front lot that was subject to periodic flooding. The living-room area, with its sweeping view of the St. Johns River, was a separate building connected by a glass enclosed "bridge" to the rest of the house. The house was demolished in 2010.

Above: The sliding glass doors opened to a view of the centuries old live oaks that graced the property as well as a view of the St. Johns River beyond. **Left:** A glass enclosed bridge connected the living room on the right to the rest of the house on the left.

O.C. Beakes Residence
1968 | Jacksonville, Florida

The three-bedroom residence with office/den is located in Venetia. Built in 1968, Hardwick designed the house for a professional couple who requested a low-maintenance, modern residence.

The design provided a high-roofed central living space with office and bedrooms in adjoining wings. The use of local building materials and the symmetrical plan of the design made possible an economical construction as well as a home of simple beauty.

Included in the design were a pool and patio overlooking the Florida Yacht Club and lagoon.

The floors were black slate, and the ceiling-high fireplace hood was made of copper. The simplicity of the interior provided a sense of space and echoed the clean lines of the exterior design.

The combination of masonry and wood materials provided a continuity and connection from the inside to the outside views of grass, water, and sky.

A garden entrance with 6-foot-high concrete wall provided privacy to the street entrance where a pleasant garden view graced the living area and bedrooms.

Top: Hanging globe lights added interest to living area with shelves of books on wall of rough sawn cedar paneling. **Middle:** Glass walls and doors overlooked pool and lagoon beyond. **Bottom, left:** Ceiling high fireplace hood of copper extended above the raised hearth of black slate matching floors. **Bottom, right:** Front entrance showing a stacked-concrete-block screening wall that protected a patio garden.

John Soles Residence

1968 | Jacksonville, Florida

A young manufacturing company executive asked Hardwick to design a bachelor residence on his large, wooded lot. The land had many live oak trees as well as a small creek.

Hardwick designed a one-story, two-bedroom house with a den. Carefully placing the structure among the ancient oaks, he used rough-sawn cedar shingles for sloped wall siding. A standing seam copper roof with dormers brought light into the house and afforded views of the trees.

During the early construction, Hardwick received an excited call from the owner. He said he was getting married, and his wife-to-be had four teen-age children! He asked if it was too late to revise the bachelor design to accommodate this change in his marital status. Hardwick hesitated before replying. Finally, he answered, "Yes. The foundations are finished and utilities are roughed in." He went on to say, "However, your lot is long enough to add a matching wing. We could locate the wing next to the kitchen." "Good," said his much-relieved client. A four-bedroom, two-bath addition with recreational room was then designed to connect with the kitchen via a covered walkway.

Top: Entrance with children's wing to the left. **Middle:** The standing seam copper roof sported slope roofed dormers over the canted shingled walls. **Bottom:** Children's recreation room and bedrooms.

RESIDENTIAL 29

Russell Newton Residence

1969 | Orange Park, Florida

On a tree-covered bluff overlooking the St. Johns River, this spacious, 5-bedroom house was constructed of used pine timbers and planks that the owner salvaged from a demolished warehouse in nearby Jacksonville.

Hardwick related that "the client called one day to see if I would look at a pile of large wood beams he had discovered. He wondered if the beams could be used in the residence he had engaged me to design. I agreed to look at the beams and give him an opinion, which was an enthusiastic 'Yes!' He said that if I could use the beams, he would buy them and have them delivered to his building lot in Orange Park where his new home was to be."

The beams and planks were of huge size. The beams, of various widths and lengths, were Southern yellow heart pine. The planks were up to 16-feet long, 12" wide and 3" thick. The condition of the beams and planks was good, with only a few defects that could be avoided by careful selection and placement.

The owner hired two men who crafted the lumber for the entire building with chain saws. Inexperienced with heavy timber construction, they became experts in cutting the framework beams to which the planks were attached and used for flooring and for hanging vertically to create exterior walls. All members were left with their weathered, rough sawn surfaces. Bolts and pegs secured fitted connections. To finish the walls, 1" x 3" battens were nailed to the plank joints inside and outside.

Before construction, Hardwick measured and catalogued each beam. He then painted numbers on their ends to ensure maximum use and appearance. Construction drawings indicated the location and exposed side of each numbered beam.

The entire house was made of used lumber except the ceilings, which were new 3" cedar decking. After ten years, the owner asked Hardwick to design an addition to the house, which he did.

Hardwick also designed a platform and stair to be built in one of the huge live oak trees in the owner's yard. Although no nails were driven into the tree itself, the platform was stable enough and large enough to hold comfortably a quartet from the Jacksonville Symphony Orchestra, who played from the platform for Newton's daughter's wedding party.

While each of his residence designs has had its own special moments of success and pleasure, Hardwick has often said that he enjoyed the challenges of this project more than those of any other house he designed.

Top: A balcony office/den, overlooked the living area with a floor to ceiling fireplace and fieldstone chimney. The glass on either side emphasized the free standing fireplace and also gave views of the trees beyond. **Above, left:** Assortment of pine beams lay helter-skelter on Newton's lot awaiting use. Sizes were 10" x 12", 10" x 10", 12" x 12", 12" x 16", lengths 8 to 16 feet. **Above, right:** The dining area was separated visually from the kitchen by a wood folding panel. The hanging light globes with red hemisphere shades were used throughout the house. The pine railings used in the house were purchased from a wrecking company's salvage yard.

Salvaged 3" planks were used for front walkway, steps and porch leading to antique door, also salvaged from a demolished building. The wood was left in its rough condition for plank and batten exterior as well as interior. The second floor balcony with wood railings was accessed from the office/den via sliding glass doors.

RESIDENTIAL 31

Thomas Madison Residence
1971 | Jacksonville, Florida

The house is located on a high bluff of the St. Johns River in Ortega, an old neighborhood of elegant, traditional homes.

The owner wanted a low-maintenance, contemporary home designed to take advantage of the expansive river view and also to fit into the tree-covered environment. Hardwick created an unobtrusive, two-story house by using natural materials and colors. The glass river-front side of the house enabled the family to watch the sunrise over the river each morning.

A 4-foot-wide exterior balcony with see-through steel railing extended across the entire second floor on the river side. At its south end, a steel spiral stair enabled family members to go back and forth to the river. And after boating or fishing, they could return to the bedrooms without entering the living area.

Stained wood siding helped the building settle visually into the environment and keep maintenance low.

The living room and dining room had sliding glass doors opening to a terrace on the edge of the high bluff, which sloped sharply down to the dock. The combined kitchen and family room had a large, centered "island" between the two areas. A copper hood offering ventilation and lighting extended over the island work place.

Above: Salvaged ornamental wood columns supported the entrance porch on the street side of house. Double casement roof shaded windows on the second floor brought light to the bedrooms. **Right:** Hardwick's renderings made before construction.

Street front

Riverfront

RESIDENTIAL

The sliding glass doors across the entire riverfront side of the house offered unobstructed views of the river augmented by the see-through steel railings. At the south end, a steel spiral stair provided easy exterior access to the second floor.

South

North

RESIDENTIAL 33

Phillip Holmberg Residence
1972 | Jacksonville, Florida

The house, located in Mandarin in a heavily wooded area, was raised above ground to compensate for the soil conditions. Ramps made entrance to the home easily accessible for the handicapped client. High ceilings in the living room had exposed wood trusses. The fireplace wall was constructed of Georgia fieldstone.

The design included four cherry-red, contemporary, hemisphere, globe lights suspended from the ceiling of the living room, serving as accent to the otherwise rustic feeling of the room.

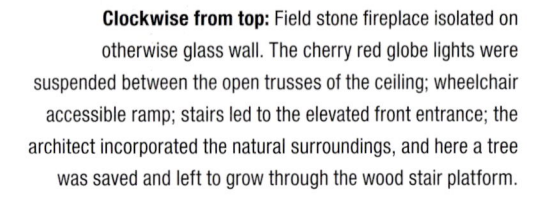

Clockwise from top: Field stone fireplace isolated on otherwise glass wall. The cherry red globe lights were suspended between the open trusses of the ceiling; wheelchair accessible ramp; stairs led to the elevated front entrance; the architect incorporated the natural surroundings, and here a tree was saved and left to grow through the wood stair platform.

RESIDENTIAL

Michael Davidson Residence

1973 | Jacksonville, Florida

A Mid-Century form was chosen for the design of this two-story house. Hardwick used precast concrete slabs to achieve simplicity and a contrasting, but compatible, presence in the dense natural environment. The clean structure blended well with lush vegetation on the site.

The slope from a terrace for outdoor living led to a deep-water dock and boathouse on the Ortega River.

The street-front entrance was accessed via a large, brick-paved terrace. The architect sized the terrace to accommodate a standard rental tent for special occasions and parties. At other times, the terrace served for parking.

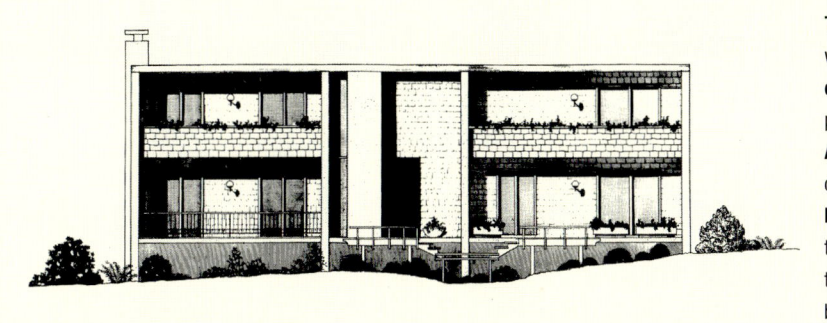

Top: River front. **Above, left:** Street elevation with terrace and parking area. **Above, center:** Living area with a ceiling of wood paneling to soften the interior concrete frame. **Above, right:** The open kitchen had a view of the wooded landscape and river beyond. **Far left:** An open tread staircase maintained the sense of spaciousness and openness of the room. Floating treads and an exposed beam ceiling contributed to the environmental compatibility sought by the architect. The natural stone floor extended throughout the living areas.

RESIDENTIAL 35

John E. Mathews, Jr. Residence
1976 | Jacksonville, Florida

The riverfront of an existing orange grove and former fish camp was the site for the Mathews' new house in Mandarin. Their children were grown, and this was to be their long-planned, private dream house.

Hardwick employed a hybrid construction of steel and wood to provide a feeling of secure spaces focused on the superb view of the St. Johns River to the south.

As President of the Florida Senate, much of the senator's time was spent out of town. He looked forward to returning as often as he could to an environment reminiscent of his boyhood years.

The architect made a special effort to merge the house design with the environment of the site with its unobstructed view of the river. The master bedroom suite was an open balcony, with bath, sleeping, and lounge areas overlooking the living area below and its 2-story wall of glass. Guest rooms and bath were on the first floor.

A small study for Senator Mathews was included in the plans and was located near the front entrance.

A gazebo equipped with bar, sink, refrigerator, and grill was constructed on the deck so that Mathews could indulge his enjoyment of cooking and grilling.

A swimming pool and patio fitted well between the house and the bluff sloping down to the dock.

Top: The riverfront of the house with walls of sliding glass doors. **Left:** Living area with open kitchen in the background. The master bedroom suite overlooked the living area. **Above:** Gazebo for grilling, complete with refrigerator, sink and bar. **Opposite page:** Photo looking down from second floor master bedroom suite with reflection of the St. Johns River in the high glass of living room. The structural engineering skills of the architect and engineering consultant were demonstrated in the hybrid construction of steel and wood offering both openness and strength to the home.

RESIDENTIAL 37

Rogers Holmes Residence
1980 | Orange Park, Florida

The home of Mr. and Mrs. Rogers Holmes just south of Orange Park has been called the "palace on pilings." The 5,000-square-foot house was built on 75 pine pilings 8 feet above ground level on seven acres bordering Doctors Lake.

The heavily wooded area of wetlands extended well into the shoreline, requiring that even the timber ramp leading to the front entrance to be raised on pilings. Travelers on the ramp often disturbed the frequent visitors of wildlife such as deer, raccoons, wild turkeys, owls, opossums and even the occasional alligator.

During construction, Hardwick took great care in meeting all environmental requirements of the Department of Environmental Regulation, which placed its approval on the completed house.

Access to the house from the street for both vehicles and pedestrians was via the extensive, lighted wood ramp that led to a parking platform constructed at the front entrance. A two-car garage was located on the platform as well as a studio/office used by Mrs. Holmes for her art consultation business.

The entire house and drive/ramp were built of pressure-treated pilings and lumber furnished by the client, who was the owner of a local lumber company. In addition to the 200-foot-long sloped, timber front ramp, a 230-foot dock was built to extend into the lake, offering boat docking and recreational space for the owners, who enjoyed fishing and shrimping.

On the lakefront side of the house, Hardwick included an extensive first-floor deck outside the living area. The design also included a second-floor balcony outside the bedrooms. All of the rooms facing the lake had sliding glass doors opening onto the deck or second floor balcony.

Throughout, the high ceilings had exposed beams and select wood paneling that enhanced the rustic effect of the interior.

Flooring throughout the home was created from carefully selected hardwood exported from South America. Mr. Holmes also chose the pine paneling for the interior of the two-story home.

One of the most intriguing features of the interior was a trophy room/office/den for Mr. Holmes. It opened from the living room through a concealed door. There the diverse career of Rogers Holmes was celebrated in trophies, photos, and memorabilia.

All the other walls and tables downstairs were adorned with the sophisticated art of Mrs. Holmes' large collection of paintings, sculpture, and glass.

Top: Sky lights afforded light to the loft area in Mrs. Holmes' office. **Above:** Front view of large parking deck showing front entrance to house and Mrs. Holmes' office opening to the left.

Left: On the north side of the house facing Doctors Lake, floor to ceiling glass walls opened onto generous screened porches. **Below:** Wood ramp leading to the garage and parking areas; the dining area opened into the living room. The wall between the dining room and kitchen was composed of a series of glass doors that opened to reveal a pass through counter to the kitchen and cabinets; living room with sliding glass doors opening to a large screened porch.

RESIDENTIAL

George Brown Residence
1985 | Jacksonville, Florida

A local investment executive and his wife requested a small, easy-to-maintain design for their empty-nest home. A wooded lot in the newly developed subdivision of Marsh Landing provided a private setting for this one-story house that was located on a dead-end street with surrounding marsh.

The front entrance to the house opened into the end of a living room with a high ceiling and with a glass wall and clerestory that faced north. The east wall had a large wood-burning fireplace with raised hearth. Sliding glass doors gave access to a swimming pool and patio.

The kitchen was "cook friendly" and was open to the living and dining areas. As was usual for his houses, the architect designed custom-built cabinets to meet the needs of the client.

A master bedroom opened onto a screened porch overlooking the backyard pool and marsh beyond. The doors to the porch were antique 12-pane French doors that folded to close.

The two guest bedrooms and bath were at the end of the house, affording privacy for guests.

Top: Extra large clerestory window facing north brought cheerful light to entire living area. **Above:** Front entrance. **Right:** The Mexican terra cotta tile flooring extended into the dining area. The marble-topped raised fireplace hearth could be used for extra seating. Matching arched doors led to guest rooms and bath.

RESIDENTIAL

Thomas Madison Summer Residence
"The Farm House"
1994 | Waynesville, North Carolina

Near the Smoky Mountain town of Waynesville is a cluster of homes known as Eagle Ridge Country Club. There, halfway up a steep slope at an elevation of 4,000 feet, is the Madisons' 4-bedroom rustic residence, designed to maximize the stunning view. The two-story home was constructed of local lumber. A huge porch wraps three sides of the house, inviting one to enjoy the mountains from one of the 21 birch rocking chairs. Stepping down from the porch, a large octagonal overlook provides space for seated gatherings and high-minded discourse.

To the east, Mount Pisgah can be seen in clear weather. On the south is a seemingly endless panorama of the Great Smoky Mountains while the western view is dominated by a deep forest of cherry and poplar trees.

The north side of the mountain had been carved out for an earlier residence that was destroyed by fire, thus creating a flat area for the main building, the gravel parking area, and the attached garage. A guest "dormitory" is above the garage. Also, opposite the

continued on next page

Above: Architect's rendering. **Right:** South elevation following a winter snowfall. **Far right:** Two of 21 rocking chairs

RESIDENTIAL 41

continued from previous page

kitchen, Mrs. Madison established an active vegetable garden.

The living and dining areas, bar, and kitchen are one large high-ceiling space accented by a large stone fireplace. Roomy window seats with built-in bookshelves are located on each side of the fireplace. Several doors open to the wrap-around porch, and all first floor windows are daylighted by skylights in the porch roof.

One guest room and a bath are located near the front door, where a powder room and the stair to the second floor are also found. A second guest room and bath and the master suite, with bedroom, sitting room, and bath, are located on the second floor. All have east or south views of the mountains through large windows.

Above: The rising sun casts patterns across the east porch. **Right:** Octagonal observation deck and overlook at southeast corner.

Left: Southwest corner. **Below:** A 144-foot porch, presenting views of the Smoky Mountains, extends along three sides. Its rough-sawn railings were constructed of native wood. The rough-sawn posts and knee braces support the heavy rafter beams of the roof. The deep porch roofs shade the windows to dining and living areas; therefore, skylights were installed over each window, giving daylight to the interior.

Left: Open kitchen with cabinet/island custom designed by the architect. **Right:** Living room with exposed ceiling beams that support the native pine ceiling. The fireplace was constructed of native fieldstone with window seats on each side.

RESIDENTIAL

44 COMMERCIAL

Commercial Projects

In the early 1950s, many of *Hardwick & Lee's* residential clients were also the rising new leaders involved in industrial and business activities of the growing city of Jacksonville. The developing reputation of *Hardwick & Lee* led many of these equally young and developing businessmen to seek the talents and new ideas of the two architects who could aid them in expanding their commercial endeavors.

When Taylor Hardwick and Mayberry Lee began their partnership practice, the two were part of a new generation of architects who were influenced by modern ideas as well as the plethora of newly developed building materials becoming available in the 1950s. Intent on avoiding a trademark style, Hardwick eagerly confronted the unique challenges of each design project, utilizing the many post-war products and techniques that were being produced.

Hardwick's purpose in his commercial design work was threefold: to design commercial buildings that met the utilitarian needs and requirements of the specific company; to create delightful and pleasurable workspaces; and to create structures that fit their physical environment. As a result, *Hardwick & Lee Architects, AIA,* was at the forefront in designing buildings for the city's flourishing business community.

Hardwick & Lee Offices

A remodeled 1909 residence

1955/1959 | Jacksonville, Florida

In 1955, Hardwick purchased a two-story frame house built in 1909 on the corner of a quiet street in Riverside. He converted the bedrooms on the second floor into one large drafting room and private offices, and a new kitchen, air conditioning, and bathrooms were also added. A commercial artist and graphic designer, John Ropp, rented the first floor, occupying that space for twenty-two years. The second-floor rooms served well for the architectural practice for several years, but as the practice flourished, more space was needed for drafting areas and design rooms.

In 1959, Hardwick purchased the house next door, which was a twin to the house where his office was located. He then built two separate second-floor bridges to connect the two buildings. One bridge was a glass walled conference room, and the other contained a private design room adjoining Hardwick's office. Below and between the bridges, Hardwick designed an open patio. To retain the character of the two buildings, he did not make any changes to the exterior of the houses but instead designed tall, perforated, precast concrete paneled walls around the two sides of the corner location.

The first floor of the second house was converted into a small furniture showroom, Atrium, Inc., the first of its kind in Jacksonville. Hardwick founded the store as a source of contemporary design furniture for his clients. Hardwick continued working in these offices until 1977 when he sold the property to a developer and thereafter continued his solo practice in another location.

The Riverside remodeled office was published in *Architectural Forum* and *House and Home Magazine*.

Above: Front entrance to the *Hardwick & Lee, Architects* offices after remodeling, showing the perforated precast concrete, paneled walls around two sides of the two houses where the offices were located. **Left:** The twin houses before remodeling. The showroom of Atrium, Inc. was originally on the right as one entered the building and was later relocated to its own building on Oak Street.

COMMERCIAL

Stairs leading up to drafting rooms and private offices were located in the front hallway. The showroom of Atrium, Inc. was on the right as one entered the building. Atrium manager Rex Dunlap stands in the background.

continued on next page

continued from previous page

Far right: Atrium conference room. **Top middle:** Porch entrance to *Hardwick & Lee* offices. **Bottom middle:** Taylor Hardwick's private office. **Below:** Patio and garden between the two remodeled houses.

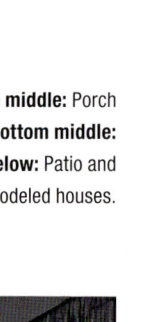

Harry James Insurance Office

1956 | Jacksonville, Florida

Hardwick designed a pair of two-story buildings located on the corner of Riverside Avenue and Fisk Street, one for use by the owner and one for a rental office. The two buildings, although separate, were visibly connected to satisfy zoning laws.

The architect chose gray bricks for the simple, handsome pair and connected the two at the entrances by a folded-plate concrete canopy. After fifty years, a new owner remodeled the buildings beyond recognition.

48 COMMERCIAL

Dr. Charles McKay Office Building

1956 | Jacksonville Beach, Florida

Dr. Charles McKay required a one-story, secure building for his one-man general practice. His lot, on a spacious and treeless stretch of vacant land in Jacksonville Beach, was ideal for a low-maintenance masonry building constructed to withstand the beach's variable weather.

The doctor had specific floor plan requirements and conveyed them clearly to Hardwick, thus creating an easy working relationship for the two men. The likable Dr. McKay became well known in his profession, and he conducted a successful practice in this fine building until he retired.

Murray Hill Barnett Bank

1957/1967 | Jacksonville, Florida

Hardwick & Lee, Architects, AIA designed the first branch office for the family-owned Barnett Bank, located in downtown Jacksonville. The new Westside Branch was on the corner of Edgewood Avenue and Kerl Street in the area known as Murray Hill. Ten years later, in 1967, Hardwick remodeled the bank to accommodate an increase in business.

The original recessed entrance wing was designed so that patrons had a dramatic view of the bank's huge walk-in vault as they approached the bank entrance. In the later remodeling, Hardwick enclosed the recessed entrance wing to provide more space for banking activities. Among other modifications, he covered the exterior glass walls of the main banking floor with aluminum sunshade grilling.

Subsequent additions and alterations were made to provide a convenient outside walk-up teller service.

COMMERCIAL

1661 Medical Building

1957 | Jacksonville, Florida

Located in a Riverside residential neighborhood near Riverside Hospital, this co-op building was owned jointly by six physicians, who were engaged in a variety of specialty practices. The completed building was published in *Architectural Record* magazine in 1958 and in the French *l'architecture d'aujourd'Hui* in 1959.

Hardwick designed a one-story scheme to house the individual practices so that they would appear as a unified group practice. The architect also sought to complement the residential environment of the triangular site, which called for on-site parking that met requirements of the city. The building's glass-enclosed single corridor was covered with a folded-plate (zigzag) poured concrete roof to break up its length and create a feeling of delight.

To resolve design complexities, the architect held many conferences with physicians of each medical specialty in order to develop an ideal floor plan for the respective practices. All the physicians' offices were to be accommodated within one attractive building; therefore, consideration was given to the relationships of the units to one another.

The structure was of reinforced concrete with Flex-Bloc walls punctuated by brightly colored Italian glass tiles and painted columns. The colorful building was an object of pride to the neighborhood.

The medical building was demolished in 2004 by developers of a multi-story residential condominium.

Top: A night view highlights the folded plate roof of the landmark building. **Right:** Offices opened onto the glass enclosed corridor. **Far right:** In order to maintain a level corridor, steps were required in only one location—at the west end.

COMMERCIAL

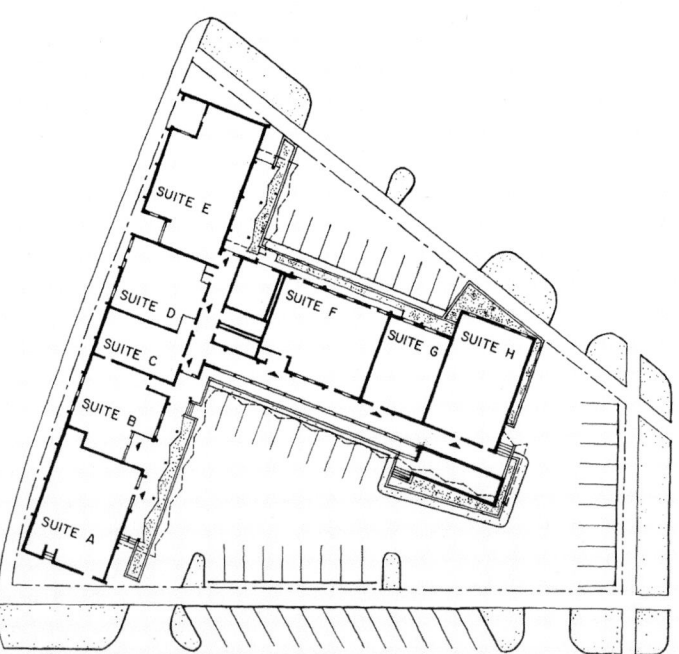

Above: The T-shaped building allowed room for parking on the triangular lot. **Below left:** The architect's drawing of the site plan. **Below right:** The steel caduceus, located at the entrance stairway, was specially designed by Hardwick for this building and was fabricated locally.

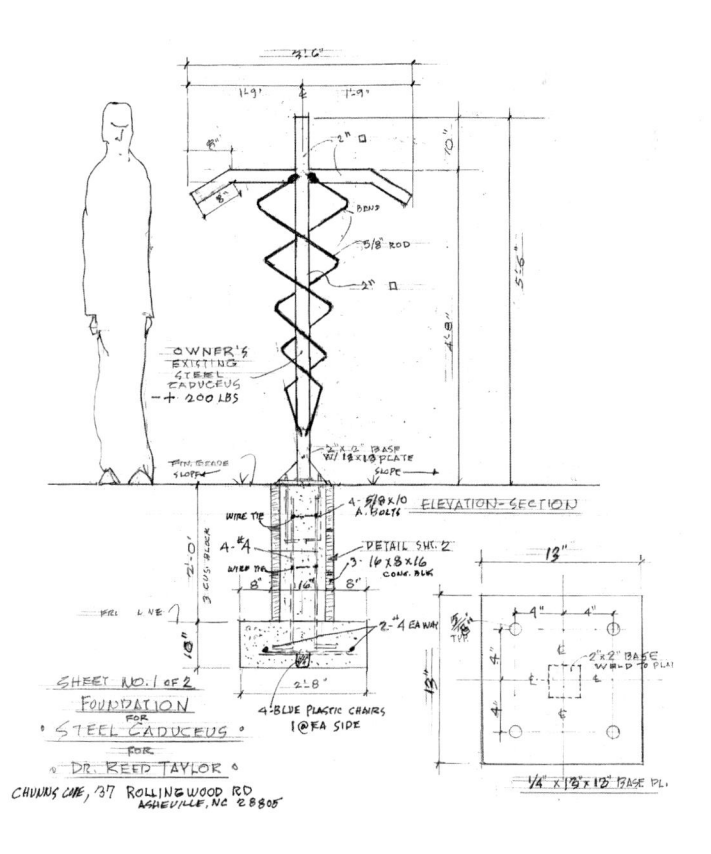

COMMERCIAL

Skinner Dairy Stores
1958 | Jacksonville, Florida

After three generations of service in Jacksonville, the Skinner Dairy owners stopped their extensive house deliveries. Prompted by the proliferation of grocery stores and convenience stores that were selling milk, the owners decided to install their own network of drive-through stores in the fast growing environs of the city.

It was important to find small parcels of land where customer traffic could approach a drive-through from two directions. After locating the appropriate sites in close proximity to residential areas, the Skinners asked Taylor Hardwick to design a prototype sales building. They wanted a small building, an eye-catcher designed to sell milk and related products, that could be operated by one attendant. The stores had to be uniformly sized for a large walk-in refrigerator and freezer. They were also required to have sliding glass doors on each side of the store through which the attendant could hand the purchased products to the customer, who did not have to leave the comfort of his or her automobile.

The Skinners started with one or two stores designed to provide ease and convenience for their customers when purchasing milk, ice cream, bread, and eggs. Within ten years, Skinner Dairy had completed twenty-one of the unique, orange-colored, drive-through milk stores. The stores had no signs; the bright orange color and innovative shape were sufficient to attract customers. The stores were an outstanding success.

In the 1990s, Skinner Dairy was sold, and the iconic, adaptable drive-through stores were put to a variety of other uses, including florist, golf instruction, bread store, dry-cleaning, coffee shop, check cashing, and others. While many have fallen into disrepair and some demolished, seventeen of the still eye-catching stores are in use in various locations of the Jacksonville area.

An interesting fact related to this commentary is that a graduate student from Jacksonville University College of Fine Arts chose to research the Skinner Dairy buildings for his graduate project. Jonathan Lux, a promising young painter now studying in London, undertook the search for the 21 recorded Skinner Dairy buildings. He then painted each of the small buildings *en plein air*. A subsequent exhibition of the several paintings was held in a Jacksonville art gallery, Brooklyn Art Center, in 2009.

Top: The bright orange dairy stores were a familiar sight throughout Jacksonville. **Above:** Hardwick, left, seen here with graduate student Jonathan Lux, who created paintings of all extant Skinner Dairy projects, circa 2004.

Three dairy stores recycled for new uses in the 1990s.

United Electric Company
1959 | Jacksonville, Florida

Hardwick & Lee, Architects, AIA, was engaged by United Electric Company to design a new showroom, sales offices, and warehouse to be located in a prominent, busy area on San Juan Avenue in Murray Hill. The client was eager to attract interest in the wide spectrum of new lighting fixtures the company offered as well as other services, such as wiring and home electrical repairs.

The architects suggested that the showroom for the new lighting fixtures be visibly separated from the warehouse and its attendant truck activities. However, a separate building was impractical. Therefore, the architect designed a second floor for the new lighting showroom and sales offices. A separate and attractive stair led to the second floor. Glass showcase windows were visible from the ground level to pedestrian and street traffic.

To soften the commercial simplicity of the exterior, Hardwick designed a colorful seven-panel screen wall. The wall was placed 6 feet in front of the building entrance where flowers and shrubs were planted and kept fresh.

The showroom's light fixtures were visible to passers-by through second-floor glass showcase windows.

COMMERCIAL

The Credit Bureau of Jacksonville
1960 | Jacksonville, Florida

This fast growing organization purchased a large property in the heart of one of the city's oldest residential neighborhoods. The address, on the corner of Duval Street and Shields Place, was across from the imposing and classical St. John's Episcopal Cathedral.

Hardwick was challenged to design a one-story commercial building that would not conflict visually with its cathedral neighbor. A large but simple, one-story brick building with no visible windows was the answer. The pointed-top brick baffle walls echoed the stained glass window shapes of the cathedral and shielded all fixed glass openings. To compensate for lack of window views, skylights and bright colors on interior walls made the workspaces cheerful.

The architect gave special attention to the brick color and landscaping to make the building a compatible neighbor to the cathedral. Sidewalks and spaces between the baffle walls were designed to afford room for flowerbeds and planters along the building walls.

Top left: The brick walls surrounded the employees' outdoor garden lounge where the Hardwick-designed Credit Bureau sign was placed. **Top right:** The triangular shapes of the brick baffle walls were the same shape as their neighbor's stained glass windows. **Middle:** Room was allowed along the sidewalks for flower beds. **Left:** The interior was roomy, airy, and cheerful with brightly colored walls in work areas.

54 COMMERCIAL

Mathews, Osborne & Ehrlich Law Offices

1960 | Jacksonville, Florida

One of the earliest skyscrapers in Jacksonville was the Lynch Building, built in 1926 with seventeen floors. When the law firm of *Mathews, Osborne, and Ehrlich* moved into the Lynch Building, the firm commissioned *Hardwick & Lee* to remodel its 15th floor office space.

Hardwick first cleared the floor of everything, including the radiators. He then remodeled the space to accommodate the required attorney offices, conference areas, and utility rooms. Hardwick also designed the interiors that included selections of furnishings, lighting, floor coverings, and the Charles Eames 12-ball classic wall clock in the client waiting room. Someone, with a whimsical sense of humor, painted the No. 5 ball red.

Above: An interior hallway led past glass-fronted attorneys' offices, utility rooms, conference rooms and library.

Above: Client reception area showing Eames clock. **Left:** The glass door and glass wall form the entrance to the law offices.

McKesson & Robbins Office and Warehouse

1960 | Jacksonville, Florida

This building complex of warehouse and offices was the regional center for national liquor distribution. The construction requirements called for a design giving special attention to security and extra structural strength. In order to soften the simple and somewhat fortress-like appearance of the building, landscape plans were provided along with an attractive pylon sign. The sign, centered on a pyramidal concrete base, included symbolic images suggesting the scope of the company's distribution to six areas.

Left: Hardwick-designed sign

COMMERCIAL 55

National Auto Insurance Company

Offices and Bathhouses

1960 | Atlantic Beach, Florida

The two-story office building was located on an important corner in the village town center of Atlantic Beach. The entire street floor of the building was devoted to offices for staff and executives. The second floor was designed for residential rental occupancy.

Eighteen blocks to the north, a private cluster of open-air bathhouses atop a sand dune was built for the use of the insurance company's employees.

A high, zigzag wall retained the dune and the bathhouses. The wall was made of reinforced concrete blocks that were filled with poured concrete and reinforcing steel.

The roof was covered with asphalt shingles in stripes of green and white and floated above the wall top so that sea breezes could enter the cubicles for natural ventilation. The attractive, louvered cubicle doors allowed both air and light to enter while affording privacy and security.

A concrete stair extended eight feet from the street level to the dune top and bathhouse floor level. Parking was available on the street along the length of the bathhouse cluster.

Above: The high zig-zag wall of the bathhouses was constructed of reinforced concrete blocks. **Right:** Air entering below the bathhouse roof provided ventilation. **Below:** Street side of the office building, located 18 blocks south, had offices on the first level and residential rental apartments on the second level.

COMMERCIAL

Atrium, Inc. and The Group Gallery

1962 | Jacksonville, Florida

Taylor Hardwick pioneered the use of professionally designed modern furniture in his buildings. With partners Charles Hardwick and William Hall, Hardwick also created the first showroom in the community to display and sell the best lines of modern furniture, fabrics, and accessories. Included lines were Knoll, Herman Miller, Dux, Richards Morgenthau, Metropolitan, Dansk, Prober, Italia Glass, and Lightolier.

Design service was also offered to customers with needs for interior planning. When required, selections and specifications were written for competitive bidding.

The furniture showroom first occupied a showroom and an office in *Hardwick & Lee*'s architectural complex. It soon, however, became very popular and needed more space. In 1962, Hardwick designed and built a separate building on Oak Street behind his Riverside office. The building was one-story with a street-front façade of three 6-foot-wide white concrete block walls. Between the walls were a spectrum yellow door and wall-to-ceiling display glass panels. Above each window, a wide panel displayed the Herman Miller colors of Alexander Girard. Hardwick employed a designer-manager, Rex Dunlap, and invited investors Charles Hardwick and William Hall to help expand the business.

The furniture showroom, Atrium, Inc., prospered and served as a franchise dealer of contemporary design furniture and accessories until 1977.

When he moved the furniture showroom to its new office, Hardwick converted the vacant space in his first floor architectural offices to a contemporary art gallery, The Group Gallery. It was operated by Hardwick's gallery partner, Jacqueline Holmes. The Group Gallery was a vanguard of contemporary art in the Jacksonville area and flourished for eight years until the property was sold.

Mrs. Holmes continued her career as an art consultant in advising corporations and collectors nationwide as well as representing artists for commissions.

Top: Oak Street entrance to Atrium, Inc, Hardwick's furniture showroom.
Left: Sign designed by Hardwick outside the offices of *Hardwick & Lee, Architects; John Ropp, Art and Advertising;* and *The Group Gallery.*

COMMERCIAL 57

Hughes Brothers Filling Station

1962 | Jacksonville, Florida

Hughes Brothers Tire Company, the owner of a prominent location at the intersection of Roosevelt Boulevard and San Juan Avenue, sought and obtained a franchise for gasoline sales. At that time, Florida law required an attendant to operate gasoline pumps. A shelter for this service and for the sale of oil and accessories was needed. The owner requested an inexpensive, yet eye-catching, small building.

An innovative plywood design was used to achieve the economical shelter. And it was with the help and ingenuity of *Hardwick & Lee*'s structural engineer Gomer Kraus that the building was assembled within a week and within the budget.

The small structure was composed of three large, boomerang-shaped sandwich frames of 2x4s covered by ⅝" plywood, each side of which was glued and screwed with 5,000 wood screws. The three forms were fastened together with 500 bolts to make a 3-sided shelter.

The unique building was an attraction for passing motorists and customers alike for several years but was demolished when the property was sold.

Above: Consulting engineer Gomer Kraus checking Hardwick's design model.

Top: Completed shelter. **Left:** The structure's boomerang-like pieces were assembled on site. **Above:** The unique and attractive 3-sided shelter attracted passing motorists.

58 COMMERCIAL

Fletcher Building

(Now Florida Physicians' Insurance Company)

1963 | Jacksonville, Florida

John Z. Fletcher and Associates, an established Jacksonville general insurance agency, had outgrown its downtown office location and sought space to expand. The Fletcher brothers, Jerome and Paul, concluded that construction of an 8-story building in a suburban location near downtown offered the best solution. The brothers planned for the insurance agency to occupy the top floor of 12,000 square feet and lease the remaining space. The site they chose for their new building was on Riverside Avenue and Post Street in the Riverside area near Five Points.

The location provided ample parking and was near the downtown business area. In addition, clients and employees alike could enjoy the serenity of the suburban area with its majestic live oak trees, low traffic, and walking accessibility to shops and restaurants.

Hardwick & Lee, Architects was chosen to design the building. After soil borings were made at the site, it was determined that the soil was poor, and a reinforced concrete mat foundation and frame would be the most practical structure to use.

The first floor walls were glass and were at sidewalk level, keeping the trees as partners. The wall panels on all floors above the first were 3″-thick precast concrete with a smooth mica-particle finish. Where panels touched at their clipped corners, they formed a typical window opening.

A glass enclosed, large conference room on the roof accented the top floor and had a remarkable cantilevered canopy of precast concrete T-beams. The canopy provided shade for the glass and the penthouse's sweeping view of the St. Johns River. The rooftop boiler flue pipe was exaggerated to become a prominent obelisk motif.

Clockwise from top right: 3″ thick concrete panels formed exterior walls; architect's rendering; the mica-particle finish of the concrete panels caused the building to glow in the sun; view of the building, located in the Riverside area, from the Acosta Bridge; the cantilevered canopy of a glass-enclosed conference room accented the top floor; detail of exterior wall panels.

COMMERCIAL 59

Office Building of Dr. Harry Good, Orthodontist

1963 | Jacksonville, Florida

First place annual Honor Award for Design from Florida A.I.A., 1964

A young orthodontist with a large practice wished to build a small building on a narrow, heavily wooded suburban lot facing a busy highway. Low building maintenance and privacy for patients were required. In addition, he requested a building that appeared dignified and disciplined yet delightful in its setting in order to alleviate the discomfort associated with the service he offered to his young patients. The frequency of the youngsters' visits and the associated feelings of apprehension were on the architect's mind as he designed the dental office.

The building that Hardwick created had stuccoed concrete-block bearing walls with ceilings of a job-laminated wood roof deck of alternating 2x4s and 1x3s. All ductwork was contained below the structural concrete floor.

The building was set back from the highway, with the parking area serving as an insulator from traffic. The remaining lot depth was preserved in its natural state for private, restful vistas.

The small 9' by 9' treatment rooms were planned with ceilings sloping up and out, away from the dental chairs and over glass walls to increase the apparent size of the spaces. In this way, patients were treated to a relaxing view of the trees and sky when their dental chairs were reclined.

Work areas with flat roofs and skylights were located between treatment rooms. The spaces were designed as laboratories with pass-through panels to the treatment rooms.

All glass facing the street was obscure, enclosing the private decks within. In approaching and entering the building, the patients encountered a variety of experiences with color and changing forms.

Top: Treatment rooms had high sloped ceilings; the laboratory prep rooms, located between the treatment rooms, featured pass-through windows to the treatment rooms. **Above left:** Entrance ramp. **Above right:** Ceiling of laminated wood roof-deck was constructed on the job. **Left:** Treatment room with view of surrounding trees. **Opposite page:** The street-side treatment rooms had walls of obscure glass.

COMMERCIAL

Holmberg Construction Company Office

1965 | Jacksonville, Florida

This general contracting company built its office headquarters just off the Arlington Expressway. The design was created to be eye-catching to passing motorists as well as secure and low-maintenance. Facing Cesery Boulevard to the west, the one-story building displayed protective, staggered concrete baffle walls constructed to shade the glass-fronted office from a harsh afternoon sun.

Above and left: All walls were constructed of stuccoed concrete block, providing a monolithic appearance.

62 COMMERCIAL

Someplace Else

Restaurant and Discotheque

1969 | Jacksonville, Florida

Built on riverfront land next to Friendship Park on Gulf Life Drive, this unique building was designed to produce income yet last just a few years until the State of Florida could use the site for a new Acosta Bridge across the St. Johns River.

The owners, brothers Jerome and Paul Fletcher, requested a low-cost, temporary building for a discotheque/restaurant and lounge. It was to be the first nightspot of its kind in the city. Before he undertook the design for the building, Hardwick, accompanied by Jerome Fletcher, toured similar establishments in Miami and other South Florida cities to appraise what was popular and successful at the time.

The Fletchers named the new discotheque/restaurant and bar Someplace Else, and it served lunch daily and dinner each night with live disco music and dancing. The completed building featured a glass dance floor with changing colored lights beneath it.

To attract attention, the sloped exterior walls of the building were sheathed with copper-faced roof insulation that shone brightly in the sunshine and sparkled at night in the light of sixteen wall-bracket globes on the entrance wall.

While traveling in France, Jerome Fletcher came upon two large, white, marble sphinxes that he purchased and shipped home to Jacksonville. The two sphinxes were placed one on each side of the entrance walkway, adding exotic distinction to the nightspot.

While attractive, the exterior copper insulation was short lived. The interiors, however, were finished with first-class materials.

Someplace Else flourished for 5 years, and then changed hands to become a restaurant named Gatsby's. Later still it was called Diamondhead Restaurant. The building was demolished in 1982 by the State Road Department.

The St. Johns River and City of Jacksonville formed the backdrop for the restaurant/discotheque, which was located on the Southbank.

Nitram Chemicals Office Building

1973 | Tampa, Florida

The client, a national manufacturer of fertilizer products, requested a new office building to be located in a Tampa industrial park. The architect designed a simple one-story steel-frame building. The concrete-block modular exterior baffle walls were designed to deter glare and dust.

Adjacent to the office building was the factory itself. The factory's 60-foot high exhaust stack had a specially constructed platinum screen designed to filter toxic chemicals from discharge into the environment. Hardwick designed the office building, and Atrium, Inc., was commissioned for the interior planning and design.

View of office building from highway showing concrete-block baffle walls in front of the glass.

COMMERCIAL

W. M. Harvey Office Building

1976 | Jacksonville, Florida

Bill Harvey, a local land developer with imagination and a penchant for new and experimental ideas, wanted a small, private office building. He did not want anything ordinary; therefore, he decided on a small lakefront lot located near a golf course and Baymeadows Road. He asked Hardwick if he had ever designed a dock house. The answer he received was, "Certainly." And so Bill Harvey, the developer of many major projects decided to build his office on a lake where no building existed.

Hardwick, another adventurer into the new and innovative, got busy designing the office building that was to be constructed on pressure treated wood pilings in the shallow lake.

The pilings were jetted by boat 20 feet into the lakebed; then the braced wood frame was assembled. Construction from that point was just like that of a conventional house—except for the peril the workers faced. They had to work on the exterior from an uneasy perch on scaffold boards lofted above the lake. Therefore, the danger of falling into the lake was real.

A short, narrow bridge connected the building to the shore and served as entrance walkway.

The frame was 2x4 studding with ⅝" plywood sheathing and rough-sawn cedar plywood board and batten siding. The building's floor plan provided a reception area, three private offices, a small kitchen, and two bathrooms.

On the high roof of the handsome building, Hardwick placed a rooster weather vane. He had purchased the antique vane during his travels in Italy and had it on display in his office. Mr. Harvey admired the weather vane, and so Hardwick, thinking that in many ways the vane was symbolic of Bill Harvey, installed it on the building's rooftop. The blending of the old with the new was typical of Hardwick's practice and, in this case, was representative of the boldness of the venture.

Top: Architect's rendering. **Above left:** Antique rooster weather vane atop the roof blended the old with the new. **Above right:** Cedar board and batten siding created a building compatible with its environment. **Left:** Bridge, with rope railings, connected the building to the shore.

COMMERCIAL

66 INSTITUTIONAL

Institutional Projects

The national prosperity that followed the end of World War II produced in the population a creative attitude and an interest in the new and modern. Thus, successful bond elections often provided the financial means for construction of larger, modern institutions with state-of-the-art facilities. As Jacksonville flourished and the population grew, so did diversity in the architectural practice of the two young architects, Taylor Hardwick and Mayberry Lee.

To meet its growing business needs, *Hardwick & Lee* invited fellow architect Duane Leuthold to join the firm. Mayberry Lee was uniquely qualified to take over school projects in both design and client contacts while Leuthold soon became manager of production in the drafting room. In addition, a long association with Gomer E. Kraus, PE, a consulting structural engineer, was of great value to *Hardwick & Lee*. Many of Hardwick's creative design ideas were realized largely through Kraus's skills and his willingness to innovate and to experiment with new construction ideas and materials.

The name and reputation of *Hardwick & Lee, Architects, AIA,* became known for its forward thinking and innovative designs, and the firm experienced a surge of important commissions in the 1950s and 60s. The award of the J.E.B. Stuart High School commission followed by the Haydon Burns Library commission were two significant steps in establishing the firm as a leader in contemporary design; thereafter, many important commissions, in both commercial buildings and educational facilities, followed.

St. Johns Country Day School
1957 | Orange Park, Florida

Founded by Dr. Edwin P. Heinrich and his wife Dorothea in 1953, St. Johns Country Day School is a non-sectarian, college preparatory school for grades Pre-K3 to 12. The campus is located in Clay County Southwest of the town of Orange Park on 26 acres of forestland near Doctors Lake.

In 1956, *Hardwick & Lee, Architects* was commissioned to design the first buildings, which consisted of the library, upper and lower school classrooms, and administrative offices.

The total enrollment at that time was 127 students. Since then many facilities have been added, and by 2013, more than 1,800 students had graduated from its expanded campus.

One of Hardwick's most pleasant memories of the design and construction of the school is the discovery of a magnificent live oak tree with branches shading a clearing near the site of the early buildings. At his suggestion, the tree became an assembly area and, on occasion, an outdoor classroom. The tree was named The Chapel Oak, and beneath its sheltering branches, assemblies are still sometimes held.

Above: Students gathered around the flag pole outside the first administration building, built in 1957. Regular morning flag-raising was conducted in the courtyard. **Right:** Tables and chairs were provided for student groupings and study in the library, which was well lighted by fixed-glass high windows and hanging globe lights. The original library space has been converted to additional administrative offices during the past few years.

68 INSTITUTIONAL

Top left: The Chapel Oak, filled with the Southern charm of Spanish moss, provided atmosphere for a variety of school gatherings under its limbs. **Top right:** A 1957 classroom building's doors opened onto the central courtyard. **Bottom left:** The hallways were lighted by suspended globe lights. **Bottom right:** Early sketch of the courtyard by the architect. The original campus was later expanded, and the number of buildings on the 26-acre campus was increased over the years to the school's present size of 14 buildings.

INSTITUTIONAL 69

Florida School for the Deaf and Blind, Crafts Building
1959 | St. Augustine, Florida

The campus of this venerable institution for the deaf and blind has been a landmark in St. Augustine for many years.

The architects were asked to design a building to house the classrooms, labs, and shops for teaching vocational skills, and it was the first building for which *Hardwick & Lee, Architects* was commissioned by the State of Florida. The State required that the new building fit architecturally with the existing campus buildings. The design, therefore, became an integral addition to a courtyard group of traditional buildings.

The interior needs for the building's teaching facilities and rooms were presented by several teachers who helped in planning the shops, not only for various trades but also for variable abilities of the students.

Top: The crafts building for the long-established school exhibited a regional character of Spanish Colonial charm and a simplicity of design with its brick columns and bricked, screen wall railing. The barrel clay tile roof added to the character and sense of tradition of the building.
Bottom left and right: The building's classrooms opened onto a veranda that extended the length of the building. Students used the sheltering shade of the oak trees, a few steps from the building, for gathering.

INSTITUTIONAL

J.E.B. Stuart High School
(Now a middle school)
1959 | Jacksonville, Florida

It was the first high school built in Duval County following World War II, and J.E.B. Stuart was also the first of *Hardwick & Lee, Architects'* several innovative major schools for the Duval County Public Schools. Located in southwest Jacksonville and planned for a student body of 1,350 students, the unusual design of this school caused much excitement and interest in the community.

Unlike previous schools, this school building was not a series of rectangular boxes under flat roofs. J.E.B. Stuart's site plan was a wagon wheel. Seven one-story spoke wings radiated from a two-story central hub, which contained student lockers on the ground floor and the library above. The seven wings, or spokes, extending from the hub were connected by covered walks circling the hub and leading to the corridor entrance of each wing and the bus loading area.

One of the wings housed the cafeteria and kitchen. Another was constructed with labs for science classes, and still another for the different administrative offices. Without load bearing interior columns, the use of classroom space in the wings was flexible.

The construction of the entire complex was of exposed reinforced concrete. The frames of each wing were poured concrete columns and beams with folded plate concrete roofs 3-inches thick and clear spanning 60 feet, the width of the wings. Ceilings were exposed concrete with skylights in the corridors.

All exterior walls were finished with brick infill and operating windows at desk height. As was the custom in those years, the school was not built with central air conditioning; the windows of each wing, however, allowed complete cross ventilation regardless of wind direction.

The durability of the construction and its low cost were remarkable. The entire school cost less than the budgeted amount of one million dollars.

continued on next page

Top: The entrance to the administration offices, located in one of the wings, or spokes, opened off the wide drive that led past ample parking areas for students, faculty and staff. **Left:** Steps led from the student locker area to the second floor of the hub where the library was located. **Above:** From the inner circle of the wagon wheel, the library that is the center of the wagon wheel, or the hub, can be seen on the right. Covered walkways extended around the inner circle for student movement from class to class.

INSTITUTIONAL

continued from previous page

Right: The folded plate roof extended over the windows to provide protection from sun and rain as well as to aid in the cross ventilation of each wing. **Middle left:** Aerial view of the unique, pioneering, wagon wheel design. **Middle right:** Skylights and windows, as well as ceiling light fixtures, provided light, airy classrooms; the operating windows allowed cross ventilation to the rooms.

Right: Taylor Hardwick and Mayberry Lee inspected progress under the folded plate concrete roof of one of the wings. The skylights were a prominent feature of the acoustical, painted ceilings and provided natural light for classrooms and corridors.

72 INSTITUTIONAL

Jefferson Davis High School
(Now a middle school)

1961 | Jacksonville, Florida

Jefferson Davis was the second high school designed by *Hardwick & Lee, Architects* for the Duval County Public Schools. It is located in the Westside area of Jacksonville and differs from J.E.B. Stuart in its site plan and structural system.

This school's structural system is conventional steel frame with brick in-fill. The plan consisted of a series of rectangular 2-story wings with exterior walkways arranged to create a campus. The building was designed with 42 classrooms for a student body of 1,200.

An unusual feature was the use of a rhythm of color panels on all the second floor walkway balconies. Also, the exterior stairways with their clothes-pin balances, or counter-weights, contributed a whimsical note.

The library was located above the bus loading area, with its roof structure suspending part of the book floor load by using exposed steel rods. This construction allowed a higher ceiling for buses and trucks.

With his ever active, aesthetic eye for unique ways of displaying artful color, Hardwick added a series of colored vinyl 2-foot round mooring floats to each rod to create an abacus effect.

continued on next page

Above: The bus loading/unloading station was sheltered by the second floor library. To achieve full height for the buses, the library was designed to be supported by framing from its roof beams with lighter framing at its floor level. This structural design required steel rods connecting the bottom beams to the top beams to transfer the library floor load (100 lbs. per square foot). The vertical framing rods were prominently displayed; therefore, Hardwick had them connected horizontally with vinyl mooring floats threaded on smaller rods. A variety of colors was used for the vinyl floats. **Bottom:** Exterior concrete walkways with steel railings extended along the second floor classroom wings and were decorated with triangular side panels of alternating colors.

INSTITUTIONAL

continued from previous page

Right: The different colored vinyl floats were fastened to the framing rods to suggest an abacus, demonstrating one of Hardwick's characteristic whimsical touches. **Middle left:** All exterior walkways were covered. **Middle right:** Exterior concrete stairs led to a second floor exterior walkway. The clothes pin-like counterbalance secured the concrete stairway to the building. **Bottom:** A covered walkway between buildings

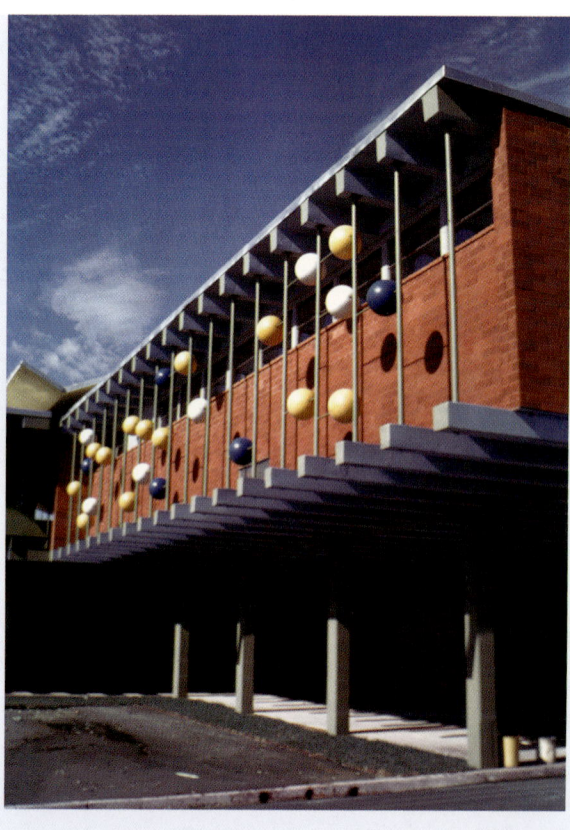

74 INSTITUTIONAL

Wolfson High School

1965 | Jacksonville, Florida

Wolfson High School was the first of the Duval County Schools to be designed with central air conditioning. All previous schools were designed for natural ventilation. Therefore, the windows were designed to provide views of the outside and to give additional light but were not required to be placed strategically for air movement.

The school was constructed on a 36-acre site and was designed to accommodate a student body of 1,570 students with parking for 400 cars. The total covered area of the school was 170,000 square feet.

The construction was steel truss roofs on steel columns and beams. Exterior walls were jumbo brick. Interior partitions were steel studs with sheetrock.

The wide, well-lighted halls, the 1,100-book library, the auditorium, and the gymnasium were student social attractions not found in previous schools. In addition, the diamond shaped roofs and ceilings of these areas were much higher than those of the classrooms. The height gave perspective and contrast to the design.

continued on next page

Top: The front reception desk. **Middle:** Wide walkways led to and from the gymnasium, cafeteria, and classrooms. The diamond-shaped roofs gave a sense of height to the otherwise low-appearing buildings. **Right:** The library was spacious and light. The tall glass end window followed the diamond shape of the roof and acoustical ceiling.

INSTITUTIONAL 75

continued from previous page

Top: The cafeteria and gymnasium stood out as taller than other campus buildings. **Left middle:** Aerial view of Wolfson campus. **Right middle:** The diamond shape of the roof contrasted with the straight brick walls of the gymnasium wing. **Bottom left:** The bus loading/unloading station was located at the front of the school.

Above: Nathan Bedford Forrest High School (now Westside High School) was built in 1966 on Jacksonville's Westside. It was designed as an exact duplicate of Wolfson High School but with an additional wing for vocational learning. At the time of its construction, the student population of Forrest was 1,800 students.

76 INSTITUTIONAL

Friendship Park and Fountain
1965 | Jacksonville, Florida

Friendship Park was developed on 14 acres of wasteland along the south bank of the St. Johns River between the Main Street and Acosta Bridges. Derelict docks and decaying buildings remained in the area where once bustling waterfront activities had taken place.

Members of the Southside Businessmen's Club were persistent in urging the city government to bulkhead the riverfront between the two bridges and create a public park. They formed an active planning and advisory group, and American Bank president Frank P. Sherman conducted many meetings to develop the design requirements for the project.

Another group concerned with community support was the Citizens Committee for Progress and Park Improvement Referendum led by Asa Gardner.

Above: The water basin was 200 feet in diameter to contain the fountain, which had three sets of jets. The central jets sent a geyser of water 180 feet skyward. There were 36 jets at the perimeter of the fountain basin and 24 intermediate jets. A cylindrical pump house with spiral walkway to its top contained the pumping equipment. The pumping velocity for each set of jets was controlled by electronic programs to create a variety of combinations. At night a variety of colored lights was employed.

continued on next page

INSTITUTIONAL

continued from previous page

The combined efforts of the two civic groups were successful in convincing the City to raise the funds necessary for creating a public park in which a fountain would be the main attraction.

As a first step, the City hired the Jacksonville engineering firm of Register & Cummings as project engineers. It, in turn, hired *Hardwick & Lee, Architects* as planning consultants for the design of the entire project. Following consultation with the various interested groups, *Hardwick & Lee, Architects* created a master plan. Architect Taylor Hardwick met with Frank Sherman's large group and explained to the members that the 14-acres of treeless land was so large that many amenities could be included as well as a fountain. He described a variety of features that could be designed to attract pedestrians as well as boat visitors, including shade and rain shelters, river-view stations, green space areas with trees, and space for games and tented activities. Small boats could be launched from the dockmaster building; large boats could be docked there also. Ample space for parking automobiles and boat trailers was included in the design.

The view of the park from both sides of the river and from the bridges was to be enhanced by the inclusion of a fountain. The fountain would have to be a giant one with a pool as large as its spout was high to contain the water. The park with its sizable fountain was to become an important landmark and attraction for the City of Jacksonville. The designers chose 180 feet for the height of the main fountain jets—the highest in the Southeast United States.

To ensure a compatible landscape, Hardwick consulted with Atlanta landscape architect Edward Daughtery, whose design and drawings were included in construction documents.

Park planners visualized a serene and delightful place for Jacksonville citizens and visitors, day or night. Strong support for these ideas was provided by the committees, and a Taylor Hardwick design was approved.

In early 1964, Register & Cummings produced engineering and construction drawings based on Hardwick's design. Public bids were taken, and before the end of the year, the contractor William E. Arnold Company of Jacksonville was awarded the job. The contract was for $1.9 million. The City Parks Department furnished all trees and plants.

Arnold's work was excellent and met the time schedule for completion, including new trees of various species planted by the City.

All went well for the grand opening on March 10, 1965, at 7:00 p.m. Huge crowds assembled on both sides of the St. Johns River as well as in the park. A two-hour display of changing colors and varying fountain heights, all with music, was the focal point of the celebratory opening.

The park has proved to be a great success for the citizens of Jacksonville. It is a popular monument for local and tourist visitors and has national and international admirers. It is still a major attraction to the skyline of Jacksonville with its amazing 180-foot water geyser, and although the park acreage has been reduced, delight in the fountain still attracts visitors from all over the world.

Top: The fountain with its outstanding water display was designed for the enjoyment of observers on both sides of the St. Johns River. **Above:** The pump house was designed with a spiraling walkway that led to the top where one could look down through a skylight into the room filled with the brightly colored pumps.

Top left: The varying heights of the jets and the changing colors of the underwater lights were controlled by electronic equipment in the pump house. **Top right:** The dockmaster's building had an observation platform on its top beneath the wide, bicycle-wheel, flat roof. The observation space was accessed by a spiral stair. Below were boat slips for docking space and pumps for gasoline sales. **Bottom left:** Hardwick designed nine mushroom-like shelters for protection from the sun and rain, each placed atop a round paving slab that was 9 feet in diameter. Each was encircled by a bench and by a planter filled with flowers. **Bottom right:** An early aerial view of the original 14 acres of park with fountain.

INSTITUTIONAL 79

Haydon Burns Public Library

1965 | Jacksonville, Florida

On a recent occasion, architect Taylor Hardwick reminisced about the construction of the Haydon Burns Public Library: "During the 18 months' construction period of the library building, I visited the site at least twice a week to supervise the execution of my design. Each time I arrived at the site, I glanced at the building on the corner diagonally across from the construction. It was the H.J. Klutho 1902 public library building, now attorneys' offices. The building had the look of strength and durability, and after more than 60 years, its timeless, classic design was still viable in the city environment.

I could not help but wonder if my library design would age as well. I felt deep admiration for Klutho's building, and I wondered if he had felt as much pride and pleasure for his design as I felt in my own. Would my forms and colors endure? And most importantly, would the new library appear inviting to the public?"

Hardwick went on to say, "Designing and supervising the construction of this public library building was a privilege and an honor. It took several years, due to the need for citizen approval of the design and bond referendum, but it was well worth the effort and the 2.7 million dollar cost."

In addition to solving the physical problems of a sloping site, sun control, the capacity to sustain 150 mph winds, as well as book storage and display, the architect was concerned with designing a bright spot in a drab urban environment. He wanted a building that would attract people and create in them an interest to enter and find out what was going on inside.

The building site sloped upward from Forsyth Street to Adams Street. The architect determined that the most desirable placement for the main entrance of the library was the corner of Adams and Ocean Streets. At this elevation, eight feet above the Forsyth Street side of the building, the entrance could be placed at the Adams Street level where pedestrian

Above: The main entrance into the library opened into the glass-enclosed reception area. **Right:** Curved insets of planters and newly planted trees along the Forsyth Street elevation afforded visual contrast to the straight, brick retaining wall. **Opposite page:** The unique cast concrete, sculptured fins were designed for wind bracing for the 3-inch thick precast concrete lift panels on the upper walls. In addition the fins provided breeze turbulence for reducing thermal transmission and for creating shadow patterns. The fins contained mica particles to aid in shedding dirt and grime. A specially created aluminum sun screen was designed for the south elevation, Forsyth Street, shown here.

traffic was high, especially during the lunch hours.

A retaining wall and fill were required at the Forsyth Street elevation in order to achieve a stepless, level main floor; thus, it became practical to include a garden to separate the south side of the building from the heavy vehicular traffic on Forsyth Street. The garden served also as an attractive enhancement to the reader's lounge planned for that area on the interior.

Hardwick's design for the 122,000-square-foot 3-story building, plus a basement, was a simple, economic, and durable reinforced concrete structure. Consulting structural engineers were Register & Cummings, who, in addition to performing structural engineering service, designed all electrical and mechanical systems. The engineers worked with Hardwick to establish a square grid-work of high strength, poured-in-place reinforced concrete columns at 25 feet on center. Floors and ceilings were poured reinforced concrete. The main floor columns were two stories for high ceilings, with stairs and a mezzanine bridge to an auditorium, Children's Department, and Art and Music Department.

All other columns were single story, including basement stack area and third floor offices. All columns at the third floor level were extended 18 inches through the roof and sealed to provide for future addition.

The east wall encased the stair and elevator tower. At the tower's first floor level, all four walls, exterior and interior, were sheathed in a colorful glazed brick abstract mural. The mural was designed by local artist Ann Williams, whom Hardwick had recommended to the City. The 1,000-square-foot glazed brick masterpiece became the focal point of the building's design.

The remainder of the east wall, including the space over the glazed brick mural, was covered by solid

continued on next page

continued from previous page

Clockwise from top: Library visitors rested on the retaining wall below the exterior of the artistic glazed brick mural designed by Ann Williams; the reference desk was centrally located on the first floor below the mezzanine; an entire wall of glass faced Adams Street, providing a full and inviting view of the library's interior.

two-story slabs composed of 3-inch-thick pre-cast, lightweight white concrete lift panels 5-feet wide and 26-feet high. To provide wind bracing, cast concrete sculptured fins, 19 feet long, were added at 5-foot centers. These fins, or ribs, were carefully sculpted to provide breeze turbulence for reducing thermal transmission and to create shadow patterns. Both panels and fins contained mica particles cast in the exposed surfaces to aid in shedding street dirt and grime.

The north side of the building on Adams Street had the same fins but with 2-story clear glass between them. The fixed glass wall of the first floor afforded pedestrians a full view of the interior of the library.

The south wall fin construction was designed with bronze aluminum sunscreen between the fins, thus shading activities without cutting out light or ventilation. The sunscreen also allowed sufficient light for the garden that ran from the glass wall of the reading room to the edge of the Forsyth Street retaining wall.

The west wall faced the back of a 15-story office building and was blank. The library's loading dock and driveway were located there.

The huge main floor spaces had 26-foot-high soaring ceilings. Hardwick wanted the entire ceiling area to have a luminous dropped ceiling rather than individual light fixtures. He discovered a new product called Squiggle Ceiling and specified that it was to be hung two feet below the structural ceiling and energized by rows of 8-foot-long florescent tubing. The Squiggle product was made of translucent white Plexiglas in 2-inch-wide ribbons twisted into a random design. The 3-foot pieces, when fitted together like a jigsaw puzzle, created a monolithic, luminous surface of unlimited definition.

The first floor reading clusters provided comfortable areas and were located at the north and south glass walls. The south reading area overlooked the garden, affording a sense of serenity to the visitor seeking a reading break.

The third floor was reserved entirely for administration offices and a processing area for the

continued on page 84

82 INSTITUTIONAL

Above left: the garden along Forsyth Street, with a second floor balcony above it. **Above right:** A reading cluster where magazines and newspapers were located for the convenience of visitors seeking a reading break. The T-Legs of the book shelves were specially designed by Hardwick in cooperation with Remington Rand to keep the bottom book shelves off the floor so that the shelves could be mopped under and around without splashing water on the books.

Left: Detail of the 19-foot-long concrete, sculpted fins extending downward on Ocean Street to meet the exterior section of the glazed brick mural, which was illuminated at night by recessed lighting.
Above: Stairs located in the glass-enclosed lobby led to the mezzanine.

INSTITUTIONAL 83

continued from page 82

entire library system. All over-looked an open-court roof garden.

When visitors entered the library, they were treated to an entirely new environment where books and people could mingle in an atmosphere of pleasant, visual surprises.

The one and only public entrance/exit was at the corner of Adams and Ocean Streets and led the visitor into the airlock glass-enclosed lobby where all noise-making activities were separated from the main floor by glass walls. The separation, however, was acoustical only and not visual. Inside the airlock was the main desk, stairs to the mezzanine bridge, two elevators, the mural walls, and a graphic directory.

When entering the main floor through the airlock's glass doors, one experienced an environment of welcome spaces and colors were bright and exciting.

The architect took great care in selecting contemporary furnishings, shelving, colors, signage, and graphics in creating unique detail leading from one space to another, to create a theme for this enjoyable environment.

At the completion of the library construction, Hardwick remarked that he had "tried to make the building, both inside and out, a place of serenity and delight where children and adults would have a memorable experience and want to return."

Above: All furnishings were selected by the architect, and comfortable, small work areas were scattered throughout the first floor. The red panels served as baffles for the return air intake of the air conditioning system. **Right:** Main entrance lobby showing a front corner of the glazed brick mural at the foot of the stairs where the elevators were located.

> "National architectural critics have agreed that the main library (the Haydon Burns Library) building is a 'modernist masterpiece'… Its designer, Taylor Hardwick, is regarded as one of the most creative Jacksonville architects in modern times …"
> —Wayne Wood, architectural historian and author, as reported in *The Florida Times Union*, January 5, 2005, *"Downtown Library needs Saving."*

INSTITUTIONAL

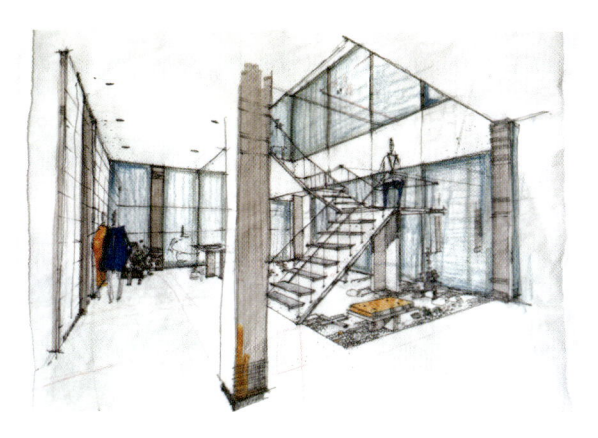

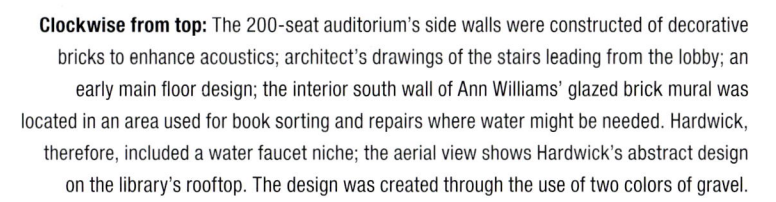

Clockwise from top: The 200-seat auditorium's side walls were constructed of decorative bricks to enhance acoustics; architect's drawings of the stairs leading from the lobby; an early main floor design; the interior south wall of Ann Williams' glazed brick mural was located in an area used for book sorting and repairs where water might be needed. Hardwick, therefore, included a water faucet niche; the aerial view shows Hardwick's abstract design on the library's rooftop. The design was created through the use of two colors of gravel.

continued on next page

INSTITUTIONAL 85

continued from previous page

Right: Small scale working models of miniature wood bricks were created by Ann Williams and were used by the mason in constructing the glazed brick walls. At the completion of the library, the miniatures were framed and hung on the walls of the 3rd floor.

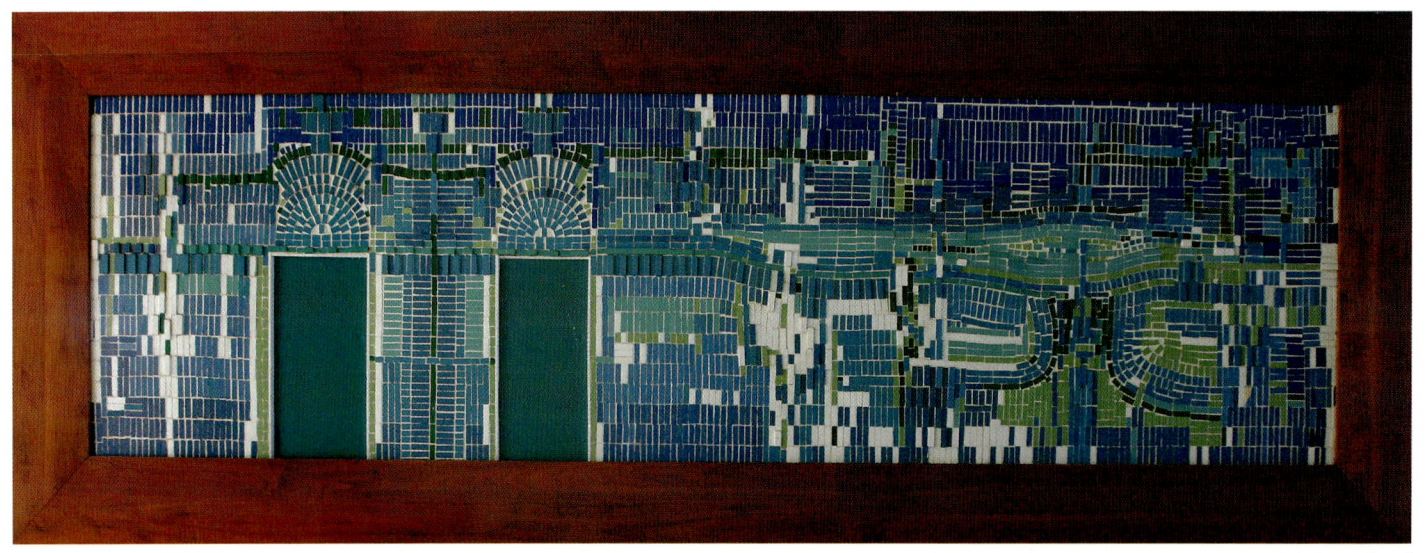

Interior east wall

A History of the Haydon Burns Library

News of the 1901 catastrophic Jacksonville, Florida, fire spread throughout the country. In New York, a young architect, H.J. Klutho determined that Jacksonville would be a rewarding place for an architect to open a practice.

Fortunately for Jacksonville, Klutho came to our town and prospered in the rebuilding of the city. He was a talented designer with proper classic training. In 1903, after many of his excellent buildings had sprung from the ashes, the opportunity arose for the City to make application to the Carnegie Foundation to participate in a competition for a new main library design. Klutho's design was chosen, and a grant for $50,000 was awarded to the City of Jacksonville to pay for the building and property.

Klutho chose a formal, neo-classic Greek temple mode for his design. It was a Beaux-Arts form, popular in 1903. Three stories tall and with capacity for 28,600 volumes, his splendid, imposing, columned masonry design remains to this day as an office building for a local law firm.

By 1957, the 21,000 square-foot Klutho library had become inadequate to serve a population growth from 28,502 in 1905 to 220,500 in 1957. The 14-member board of library trustees decided to provide a newer library service to the public. Their first step was to commission a library consultant, John Hall Jacobs from Atlanta, to make a study of the current needs and future population growth. His report also included

The 1905 Jacksonville Public Library building was designed by H.J. Klutho and was located diagonally across from the Haydon Burns Library. The building is now occupied by a Jacksonville law firm.

service to suburban communities as well as Jacksonville's urban needs. The report specified a new building of a minimum 135,000 square feet, designed to accommodate 550,000 volumes—more than ten times larger than the Klutho building of 1905.

After studying downtown traffic patterns, both pedestrian and vehicular, Jacobs chose the full-block site of the then existing City Hall, which was also designed by Klutho in 1901. That classic, domed civic building was outmoded and was to be demolished. A large hotel, the Windle Hotel, was also located on the property and was scheduled for demolition in order to provide sufficient space for a building that would meet the city's requirements of a

86 INSTITUTIONAL

Exterior east wall

new library. In 1960, the Library Trustees commissioned *Hardwick & Lee, Architects* to design the new library.

Construction on the new library began in 1964 following a bond campaign to fund the new library, and the building was completed in 1965.

After Taylor Hardwick made visits to "numerous libraries across the southeast," he presented a design for a "three-story library with two additional stories underground." (Subsequently, the decision was made for only one additional story underground.) Hardwick described the new library as "designed to be airy, inviting, and cheerful." The building was "to be constructed of reinforced concrete, large glass panels, and sunscreens, and featuring large open spaces on the inside to maximize flexibility of use and to provide a greater sense of opening."

"The approximately $3.9 million necessary to construct the new main library, as well as a new branch facility (Dallas Graham Library) … was incorporated into a larger $7.65 million bond issue that also included a new waterfront park with marina on the south bank and a new river front parking lot behind the East Bay Street city hall."

"On April 3, 1962, 10,046 freeholders approved bonding the City for $7.65 million to fund all three projects. The proposed construction of a new library received the greatest mandate … The Auchter Company of Jacksonville started construction of the new library in March of 1964 with the official opening on November 28, 1965." The result was a 122,000-square-foot, 3-story building with one underground floor. The design further included plans for an optional fourth story that could be added at a later date if desired. The total cost of the library was $2,477,000.

"… it has been the practice of the Planning and Development Department to evaluate the builder, designer, or architect of proposed landmarks based on their contribution to the development of the City. At the same time, the design and construction of the proposed landmark are evaluated with regard to how well they represent the work and contribution of the builder or designer over the scope of their career. This contribution can reflect their use of distinctive materials, styles, or methods of construction, quality and uniqueness of design, or visual, social or economic impact on local communities, neighborhoods and institutions. The body of work produced by Jacksonville architect, Taylor Hardwick, over a fifty-year period stretching from 1952 to 2001, meets this criterion based on a multitude of factors including style, method of construction, quality, and uniqueness of design. The significance and importance of his work to the city was particularly noted in 1999 when the Jacksonville Chapter of the American Institute of Architects presented Taylor Hardwick with the Henry John Klutho Award, which, 'is given in recognition of life-long commitment to design excellence, advancement of the profession, and the enhancement of the built environment.' The Haydon Burns Public Library is commonly recognized as his most significant work, not only because of its very public location and use, but also because it embodies so well the unique elements of design that have come to characterize the work of Taylor Hardwick."

(Excerpted from *Designation Application and Report of the Planning and Development Department of the City of Jacksonville Regarding Proposed Designation of the Haydon Burns Public Library, 122 North Ocean Street, LM-09-02* [Prepared in accordance with Chapter 307, city of Jacksonville Ordinance Code, March 25, 2009] pages 3 - 7).

Library's Original Architect Comes Back to the Building

This article, written by Mary Kress Littlepage, appeared on the Jessie Ball duPont Center website in November 2013. Photos by Robin Clark.

Renowned architect Taylor Hardwick toured his favorite project, the Haydon Burns Library, in late October, taking the opportunity to revisit his past and glimpse the future. In both respects, he liked what he saw.

"I'm pleased," he said after the two-hour tour. "I'll go home rejuvenated."

Hardwick, now 88, designed the library for the City of Jacksonville in the 1960s. It opened in 1965 and for 40 years was a focal point of downtown Jacksonville.

Abandoned by the City in 2005, the building sat vacant until June, when the Jessie Ball duPont Fund bought it with the intent of converting it into an office and meeting center for area nonprofit and philanthropic organizations.

Sherry Magill, president of the Jessie Ball duPont Fund, invited Hardwick to walk through the building with Will Morris of KBJ Architects, who will handle the renovations.

Hardwick's enthusiasm for his favorite project has not dimmed with the years. He arrived with a satchel of black and white photographs, sketches and color drawings of the building. He recalled a wealth of details, from the source of the tiles in the Forsyth Street garden to the rationale for certain window features. He explained the unique lighting in the second-floor theater and the story behind placement of the sink in the tile mural on the first floor. As he walked around the administrative offices on the third floor, he ticked off who occupied which space.

He clearly was relieved and pleased that the building is in relatively good condition, given how long it has been vacant. "I don't want to say I was nervous, but…," he said.

Mary Kress Littlepage courtesy of the Jessie Ball duPont Center.
Photographs by Robin Clark courtesy of the Jessie Ball duPont Center.

"The contractor who built this building [the Auchter Company] did a marvelous job and the superintendent was a gem," Hardwick said. "The whole building is high-strength concrete …The building is here to stay."

Magill and Morris explained to Hardwick the ways in which they envision changing the interior spaces to accommodate offices for nonprofits and gathering spaces for meetings, events and community convenings.

"We love your building and we are going to take good care of it," Magill said.

"I think it's wonderful that you want to do this," Hardwick said. "It's been threatened so many times … I used to have black hair! This is very exciting … it's very good."

Right: (L to R) Taylor Hardwick, Will Morris and Sherry Magill discuss plans.

88 INSTITUTIONAL

Little Hall: Classrooms, Lecture Halls, Faculty Offices
1965 | University of Florida, Gainesville, Florida

Little Hall, named for Winston W. Little, who founded and served as dean of the university's first college, is located directly behind the University of Florida's administrative building, Tigert Hall. The design program that the college staff presented to the architect called for a low-maintenance 4-story, 79,000-square-foot classroom building, and most importantly, a building with flexible teaching spaces and faculty offices.

Hardwick & Lee, Architects along with Gomer Kraus, consulting structural engineer, began this design by making a series of soil borings in order to determine load-bearing capacities of all sections of the site. The areas in and around Gainesville are noted for subterranean lime rock caves and streams.

Hardwick developed a unique scheme that involved a 4-story reinforced concrete building supported by 10 exterior towers, four on each side to support the clear span floors and two on each side for the entrances.

The exterior towers were necessary in order to provide the desired columnless interior flexibility. Therefore, the massive exterior columns carried the full brunt of the building's load and made the soil borings important. Each tower was 66 feet high and 20 feet wide, except for the wider entrance towers. Each was made of two 8-inch thick, reinforced concrete columns. The width of the towers' columns sloped outward at the bottom to form a boot designed to provide wind resistance. The bottom-sloping design resembled the root structure of a type of tree that grows abundantly in Costa Rica, the Pochote tree. Between the two tree-like columns of the eight supporting towers, a full-height brick wall enclosed utility rooms, stairs, and bathrooms on each floor on each side of the building.

The towers, supported load-bearing beams and slabs spanning across the width of the building. Student traffic was moved on several exterior stairs and along the 9-foot-wide open walkways.

The large space of each floor's rectangle could be subdivided with moveable partitions to accommodate various sizes of classrooms. The classrooms were thus developed without limits in size and usage. The fourth floor was devoted to faculty offices, and two lecture halls were placed on the first floor. The total seating capacity of the building was 1,500.

Top: The southeast elevation reveals the concrete and brick structure's unique design that not only fit among the more traditional buildings on the campus, but also stood out as an example of Mid-Century Modern architecture. **Above:** A first-floor lecture hall. **Left:** Wide concrete paths around and through the building allowed student walkers as well as bicycle riders easy access to corridors.

continued on next page

Top left: Full-height brick walls on each end enclosed stairs, restrooms, and utility rooms. **Top right:** The architect's rendering shows the front entrance leading to the main hallway that extended from the front to the back entrance, which was an exact replica of the front facade. **Bottom left:** Copy of the letter that Hardwick received from Robert Mautz upon completion of Little Hall. **Bottom right:** The base of each huge supporting tower's columns sloped outward to provide wind resistance.

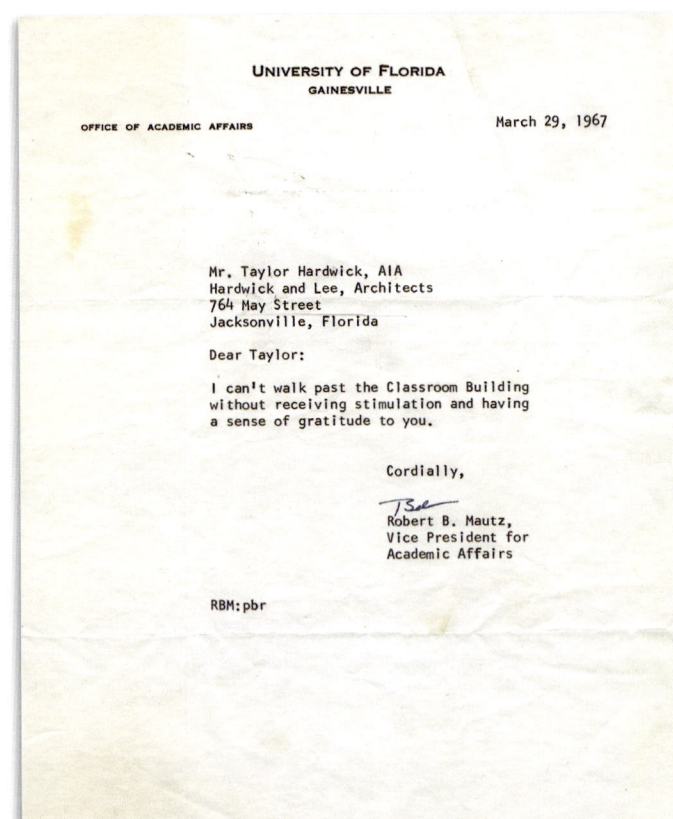

UNIVERSITY OF FLORIDA
GAINESVILLE

OFFICE OF ACADEMIC AFFAIRS

March 29, 1967

Mr. Taylor Hardwick, AIA
Hardwick and Lee, Architects
764 May Street
Jacksonville, Florida

Dear Taylor:

I can't walk past the Classroom Building without receiving stimulation and having a sense of gratitude to you.

Cordially,

Robert B. Mautz,
Vice President for
Academic Affairs

RBM:pbr

---

90 INSTITUTIONAL

Top left: The towers supported load-bearing concrete slabs and were placed against the open walkways. **Top right:** The Pochote tree's outward sloping base and roots enable it to withstand hurricane strength winds. **Left:** architect's scale model of Little Hall.

continued on next page

INSTITUTIONAL 91

Tall trees and broad paths surrounded Little Hall, adding to the majestic yet simple design.

Jacksonville Art Museum
1967 | Jacksonville, Florida

In 1964, the Board of Trustees of the Jacksonville Art Museum sold its home on Riverside Avenue to a developer. The house, built in 1906, had once been the residence of prominent attorney Francis P. Fleming, Jr. and had been owned by the art museum since 1947.

To keep the homeless institution alive until the new building could be built, Hardwick located an abandoned grocery store that was suitable for use by the museum during construction of its new home. Members gutted and cleaned the store for studio and film space in the temporary location named Studio M that, as it turned out, lasted two and a half years.

The museum commissioned architects Robert Broward and Taylor Hardwick, both long time supporters of the art museum, to collaborate on a design for a new building to be built on spacious property donated by Mrs. Ira Koger. The property site was on Pottsburg Creek in South Jacksonville—an ideal location.

The new museum was spartan in design but attractive and efficient. The building extended the entire length of the property. The public entrance to the museum on the long, west street wall was of beige brick with a splendid half-circle arch. The arch was constructed of soldier bricks matching the wall's cornice trim.

Up seven steps from the sidewalk and through the arch was a full width glass entrance, recessed eight feet to provide shelter for visitors during rains. The glass doors led into a wide reception area with a counter on the right. Beyond the counter were the office and administration suites.

Opposite the counter was a generous lounge and fireplace. The east, or back, wall stretched the full length of the building. It had floor to ceiling glass providing a view of Pottsburg Creek and trees beyond a paved patio. As one walked along the hallway, he or she passed by a delightful view on one side and entrances to various studios and lecture rooms on the other. A variety of uses was possible for this lengthy skylighted space because the concrete structure was a clear-span building with no interior load-bearing partitions or columns.

The handsome, new building served well for a number of years until the Board of Trustees decided to sell the building and move the museum downtown to a remodeled office building facing Hemming Plaza. The name of the museum is now Museum of Contemporary Art Jacksonville (MOCA).

Top: The graceful half-circle arch of the front entrance was trimmed with soldier bricks that matched the museum's cornice trim. **Middle:** Broward's rendering. **Above:** The first home of the Jacksonville Art Museum was a 1906 house located on Riverside Avenue.

INSTITUTIONAL

NOTEWORTHY

Noteworthy Selections

The diversity of Taylor Hardwick's creative talents became apparent in his boyhood. His early interests, what Taylor referred to as "making things," were first noticed by his parents. The "things" were not constructed from the usual factory-made assembly games and toys that were popular then and now, but rather the sorts of things that he observed adults creating, or building, as they went about their necessary chores or engaged in their hobbies.

Whenever he had the chance, Taylor was designing and building. In an early shop class, he was given the materials and instructions to build a birdhouse. He completed the assignment and then spent the next class remodeling the birdhouse. He was fascinated with mechanics as well as carpentry and masonry. He built his own motorized scooter as a boy and later tinkered with his own cars. As an adult, Taylor redesigned a 1961 Ford Thunderbird. A mechanic with Pedrick Motor Company performed the transformation under his supervision. The redesigned vehicle was fondly called the Cinderbird and afforded Taylor a number of years of pleasure before he sold it to his godson. He learned photography from his cousin, a professional photographer, and developed his talents in that area, progressing later to movie making. Taylor also painted and sculpted, finding pleasure in both art forms, but his main love was architecture.

The fruits of his creative talents have been both whimsical and serious in character. Often one can discover the inclusion of an amusing bit of design in an otherwise somber undertaking. But always he has taken his architecture seriously. He appreciates both the aesthetic and utilitarian aspects of his buildings, and he has always kept his focus on the needs of his clients.

The creative projects Taylor Hardwick engaged in are too numerous to name, but in the Noteworthy section, one can catch a glimpse of the wide range of his talents.

Noteworthy Selections

1 Taylor wielding the camera in a junkyard, one of his favorite subjects. 2 Taylor rides the motor-scooter he designed and built as a boy. It was propelled by a Maytag one-cylinder gasoline engine, 1936. 3 Taylor in his 1939 British MG Midget convertible. 4 The barn of Hardwick's boyhood home with its smaller companion, the corn crib that Hardwick used as a model for many of his later designs, 1940. 5 Fondly dubbed "The Cinderbird" by friends and neighbors, Hardwick's rebuilt design of a 1961 Ford Thunderbird was a popular sight in his neighborhood. The family nickname "Cinder" originated during his childhood and has followed Hardwick throughout his life. 6 While in college, as his senior thesis, Hardwick created the model of a Catholic church that followed the basic design of the corn crib of his boyhood home, 1949.

96 NOTEWORTHY

7 Hardwick in 1966 with glazed bricks left from the Ann Williams library mural. **8** The unique cover for a residence sprinkler pump was a replica of a small church, complete with belfry, designed and built by Hardwick in his workshop in 1983. **9** Displaying another touch of whimsy to a serious subject, Hardwick creatively offered a solution to the vulnerability of a city's outstanding skyscrapers. He visualized an entire community of low-rise towers. He named his structure "A Model Monument for 9-11", 2001. **10** The framed wall ornament was designed and built from 65 bottle tops in 1995. **11** Taylor Hardwick in his workshop in 1983.

NOTEWORTHY

Noteworthy Selections

12 One of several small tables built by Hardwick in his workshop and given to his client. This one had a tile-top that was created from tiles left on a client's construction site. **13** Hardwick created the 16" x 24" mirror frame from dozens of tiny spindles, 1995. **14** Hardwick created the two candle holders in 1982 from old cast iron washers that he found in a local junkyard. **15** While supervising the construction of the Madison home in North Carolina, Hardwick displayed his sense of humor by building a "friendly face" from the cut of a cherry log, 1984.

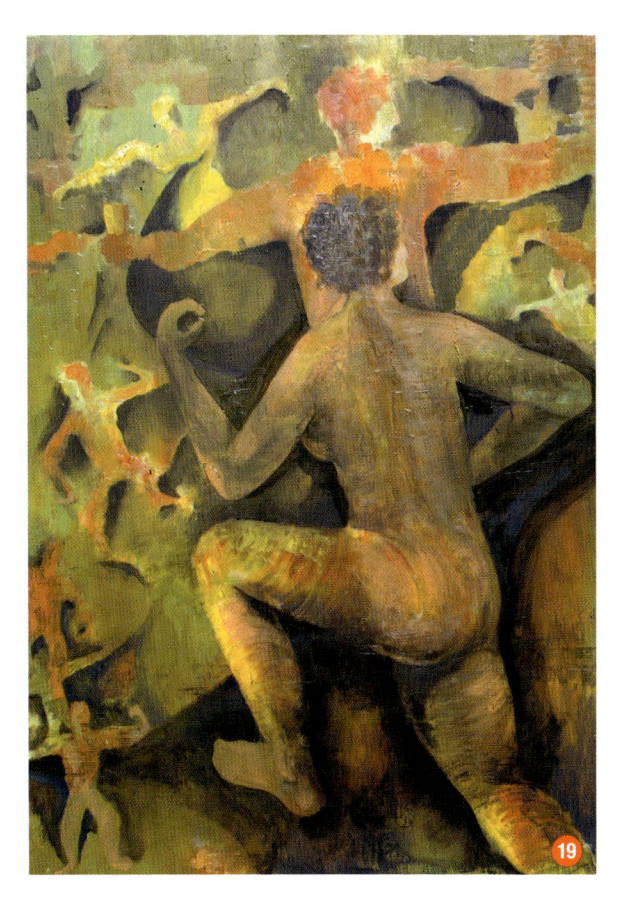

16 A 13-inch high polished bronze casting of an abstract female figure sculpted by Hardwick in 1947. **17** One of several bowls created by Hardwick in his workshop was made from cherry wood from a North Carolina building project. **18** A salvaged, antique frame was reborn in 2010 as a table tray holding a collection of old keys embedded in clear plastic. **19** *Welcome to the World,* oil on plywood, 48″ x 36″, painted by Hardwick in 1962.

Noteworthy Selections

20 In his workshop, Hardwick designed and built a ceramic tile coffee table as a gift to a client, 2005   **21** As a gift for his daughter Margie, Hardwick designed and built this whimsical coatrack in 1975.   **22** In 1987, Hardwick built a china cabinet with doors made from two salvaged pine window sashes. The cabinet is 6'4" tall and 4' wide and has adjustable shelves and internal lighting.   **23** After measuring a client's antique wall shelf, Hardwick built a new version in his workshop.   **24** Hardwick designed and fashioned a Williamsburg frame with his scroll saw to create an intriguing frame for a classic beveled mirror.

25 The sketch for a sign was completed by Hardwick for a developer, circa 1980. The sign was to be used at the entrance to the subdivision. **26** Dissatisfied with a plain pressure-treated pine post for his backyard hammock, Hardwick exhibited his creativity by designing and building an interesting adornment for his post, 1982. **27** Another sketch of a sign presented to the same developer that was rejected in favor of the first sign. Hardwick designed many signs for clients for use at their places of business as well as signs for construction sites.

Noteworthy Selections

Hardwick & Lee always required in their bidding documents that the contractor was not to display his own job sign nor that of his sub-contractors. A cost allowance was included in *Hardwick & Lee*'s specifications for the construction of a job-site sign with a design provided by the architect. Each job site therefore, displayed a unique Hardwick designed site sign. **28** The Credit Bureau. **29** Office Building for Dr. H. C. Good, Jr. **30** Forrest Senior High School. **31** Entrance sign to *Hardwick & Lee* offices.

32 – 36 *Hardwick & Lee, Architects* designed signs for various construction sites.

Noteworthy Selections

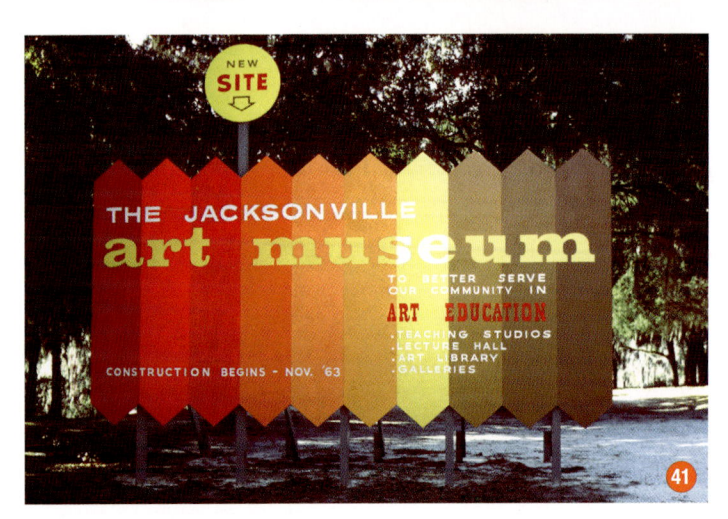

37 Sign for Atrium, Inc. **38** Holmes Lumber Company sign on Roosevelt Blvd. **39** Sign designed for *Hardwick & Lee* office site. **40** Jefferson Davis High School construction site sign. **41** Sign designed for the Jacksonville Art Museum's construction site.

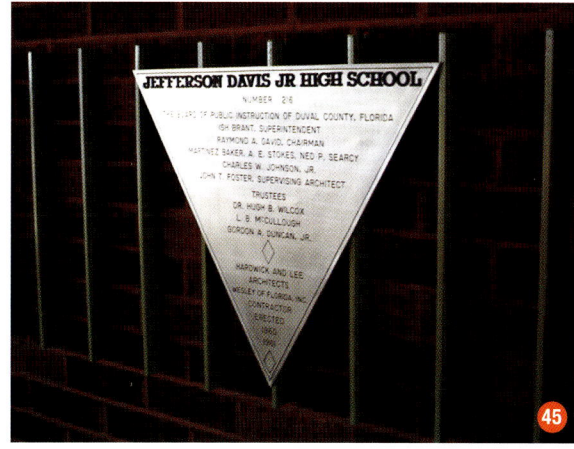

42 Haydon Burns Library construction site sign. **43** J.E.B. Stuart construction site sign with red squiggly line symbolizing the folded plate roof top. **44** Signs designed for Fletcher Building, advertising space for rent.
45 Jefferson Davis sign indicating responsible public school employees as well as architects.

Noteworthy Selections

46 - 47 The sunken conversation circle was an extended part of the patio for an Ortega riverfront residence. **48** Gomer Kraus's office building was located behind *Hardwick & Lee, Architects* in Riverside. Hardwick designed the remodeled entrance in 1962. **49** The circular tool storage house with conical roof was constructed of brick in 1959 for Dr. Champ Taylor.

50 Hardwick designed the patio for his Ponte Vedra residence in 2008.   **51** Hardwick in his residence gallery.   **52** Aerial photo of the "Super Pool" designed for a Baymeadows development in 1980.   **53** Hardwick at work in his residence studio. 2009

1999

THE JACKSONVILLE CHAPTER OF

THE AMERICAN INSTITUTE OF ARCHITECTS

PRESENTS THIS

HENRY JOHN KLUTHO AWARD

TO

Taylor Hardwick, AIA

Henry John Klutho was one of Jacksonville's most talented and prolific architects. During a career that spanned over six decades, he created numerous works of consistent high quality that, to this day, continue to be a significant part of the City's architectural fabric. In the spirit of this accomplishment, this award is given in recognition of life-long commitment to design excellence, advancement of the profession and the enhancement of the built environment.

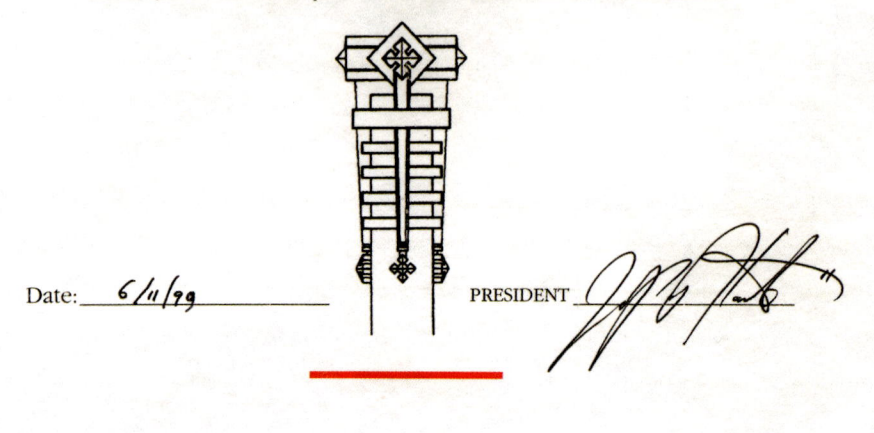

Date: 6/11/99   PRESIDENT

In 1999 the Jacksonville AIA presented the Klutho Award to Taylor Hardwick in recognition of his architectural contributions to the City of Jacksonville, Florida.

Acknowledgements

This book is the fulfillment of a long-held dream and represents the major passion of my life—creating and building something new, unique, that no one before has created. Nevertheless, the book would not have been possible had it not been for those who have provided support and help along the way. They are many.

Kenyon Drake gave me the opportunities and the confidence to develop my own ideas. He taught me the meaning and importance of ethics in business, and his encouragement gave me the motivation to set out on my own. I will always be grateful to Mr. Drake for believing in me.

I cannot overlook the people who worked with me and for me in my office and who contributed significantly to my success. Among them were **Nanan Lee**, **Harriett Hodgson**, **Gay Hardwick**, and **Meg Alward**.

The draftsmen who worked alongside me and endeavored to transfer my ideas to paper were invaluable to my career as well.

My appreciation and thanks are extended to my colleague and friend, architect **Duane Leuthold**, who was charged with managing the drafting room at *Hardwick & Lee*. He contributed advice and instruction, not only to the young draftsmen, but to me as well. His precise construction drawings and his suggestions, derived from his penetrating sense of design, were always welcomed.

I owe thanks to the many contractors, who, over the years, executed the designs I presented to them. **Gomer Kraus, PE**, consulting structural engineer, particularly stands out as one who worked with *Hardwick & Lee* on many projects and whose willingness to experiment and try new ways of construction helped many of my projects reach fruition.

I am indebted to **Jonathan Lux**, who researched my career and buildings for his graduate project and shared with me the results of his study.

Many thanks to **Paul Karabinis** for the recording and cataloging of all the photographs of my work, and thanks as well to **FotoTechnika** for their work in restoring beauty to old photographs.

Architect and author **Glenn Hettinger, AIA**, was generous in sharing his book-producing experiences with me. I remain grateful for his being so forthcoming in ideas and suggestions.

The contributing photographers, both professional and amateur, have been indispensable to the completion of the book. **Alexandre Georges**, who photographed my first home designs in 1954, deserves special thanks, for he returned to Jacksonville each year for 25 years to photograph my buildings. Both his loyalty and his expertise have been of inestimable value.

Several people helped me put the book together and patiently read over and over the accompanying text. Among them is my attorney and good friend, **Jeffrey Dunn**. He read text of every page and made comments that were both helpful and insightful. His advice and his experience served as encouragement throughout.

Wayne Wood has been an invaluable source of knowledge and generous with his help and suggestions. I have greatly benefited from his counsel and the interest he has shown in this undertaking.

Architect and friend **Michael Dunlap** worked with me on every page, helping in photograph selection and technical writing. Many times, he went to the site with his camera and took the needed photographs himself. He was a dependable, loyal, and an essential assistant to the book project. The book would not have been completed without him.

And of course, **Jill Applegate**, the talented and able graphic designer, who so good-naturedly discerned what I wanted and where I wanted it in the book, and who was available throughout the project. She remained helpful and patient no matter how many times I might have changed my mind. Her professionalism and artistic judgment laid the foundation for the development of a book I could not have produced without her.

Members of my family were supportive and helpful throughout. My nephew **Adam Groff** read text and studied organization, offering critiques and suggestions that were not only helpful, but reflected a younger, upbeat way of seeing the book. My wife's son **Mark Alexander** provided help in seeking permissions for reprinting. My wife's daughter **Laura Alexander** provided some much needed substantive analysis of the text, and her comments and insight aided us in the tedious task of cutting. My daughter **Margie Hardwick** was, as usual, supportive and helpful in tangible ways. Her cheerful encouragement helped me to stay focused and on task. My wife **Jo** was and continues to be a source of love and encouragement. She was essential to the writing as well as helpful in every other aspect of the book's production. She has remained positive and encouraging throughout and has worked diligently to make sure the printed words were as they should be.

Lastly, I remember my partner **Mayberry Lee**. He and I worked together in friendship and with professional respect for sixteen years. He was always a voice of reason, and his resourcefulness, knowledge, and talents were invaluable to the success of our shared work. In honor of his memory and our friendship, I dedicate this book to him.

—Taylor Hardwick, AIA, Emeritus

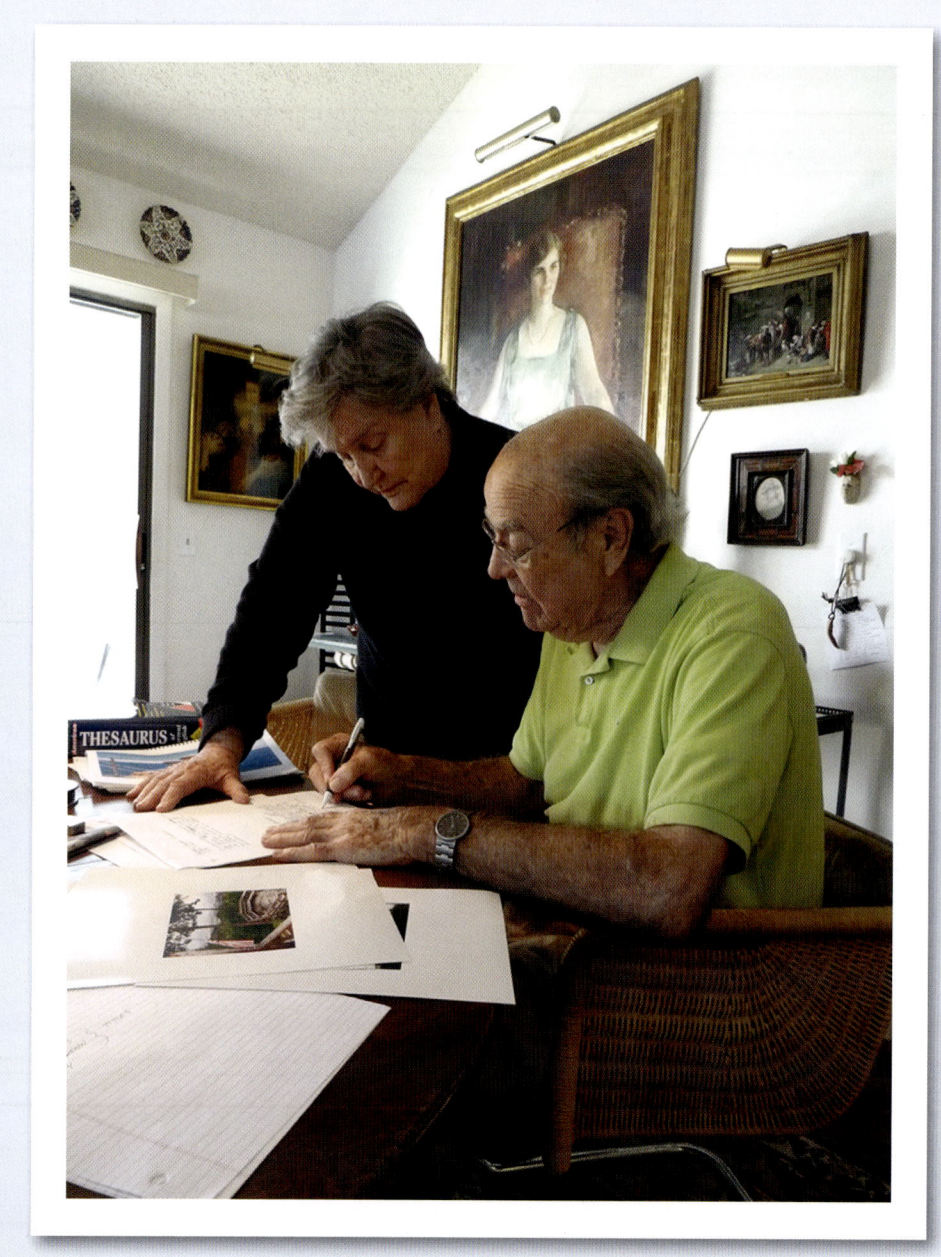

Jo and Taylor Hardwick at work in his residence studio, 2013

110 60 YEARS OF DESIGN

Credits

Book design

Jill Applegate Design

Photo and rendering credits

Page ii: Taylor Hardwick
Page 1: Ed Fritsh
Page 2 - 3: Homasassa, Green Derby: Taylor Hardwick; Six Jaxons: Times-Union; May and Fisk Street office: Elsner; Atrium, Inc.: Alexandre Georges
Page 4: Phil Kafka
Page 5: Alexandre Georges
Page 6: Michael Dunlap
Page 8 - 10: Taylor Hardwick
Page 11: Michael Dunlap
Page 12: Taylor Hardwick
Page 14: Patio photo: Alexandre Georges; screened porch photo: Milton H. Greene
Page: 15: Firebrick photo: Rudi Rada; bedroom photo: Alexandre Georges; street elevation photo: Milton H. Greene
Pages 16 - 22: Alexandre Georges
Page 23: Top photo: Alexandre Georges; bottom photo: Taylor Hardwick
Pages 24 - 25: Alexandre Georges
Page 26: Left photo: Taylor Hardwick; right photo: Alexandre Georges
Pages 27: Wade Swicord
Page 29: Alexandre Georges
Pages 30 - 31: photo of pine beams: Taylor Hardwick; all others: Alexandre Georges
Pages 32 - 33: Alexander Georges
Page 34: Taylor Hardwick
Page 35: Kathleen McKensie
Page 36: Alexander Georges
Page 37: Michael Dunlap
Pages 38: Top photo: Taylor Hardwick; bottom photo: Gene Heape
Page 39: Taylor Hardwick
Page 40: Taylor Hardwick
Page 41: Winter scene: Julie Madison; rocking chairs: Jo Hardwick
Page 42: East porch photo: Jo Hardwick; all others by Taylor Hardwick
Page 44: Rendering by professional rendering company
Page 46: Top photo: Alexandre Georges; bottom photo: Elsner
Page 47: Alexandre Georges
Page 48: Photos of *Hardwick & Lee* offices: Alexandre Georges; Harry James Insurance office: Taylor Hardwick
Page 49: Dr. Charles McKay: Dean's Studio; Murray Hill Barnett Bank: Alexandre Georges
Pages 50 - 51: Alexandre Georges
Page 52: Photo of store: Taylor Hardwick
Page 53: Top left: Jonathan Lux; top middle: Michael Dunlap; top right: Taylor Hardwick; United Electric Company: Taylor Hardwick

Page 54: Top left: Taylor Hardwick; top right and middle: Michael Dunlap; bottom: Alexandre Georges
Page 55: Alexandre Georges
Pages 56 - 57: Taylor Hardwick
Page 58: Top photo: Alexandre Georges; all others: Taylor Hardwick
Page 59: Photo from the Acosta Bridge: Taylor Hardwick; all others: Alexandre Georges
Pages 60 - 62: Alexandre Georges
Page 63: Rendering by professional rendering company
Page 64: Alexandre Georges
Page 65: Taylor Hardwick
Page 66: Wade Sweicord
Pages 68 - 69: Alexandre Georges
Page 70: Taylor Hardwick
Page 71: Alexandre Georges
Page 72: Photo of folded plate roof and classroom: Alexandre Georges
Pages 73 - 75: Alexandre Georges
Page 76: Nathan Bedford Forrest High School photo: Michael Dunlap; all others: Alexandre Georges
Page 77: Taylor Hardwick
Page 78: Judith Gefter
Page 79: Top right: Taylor Hardwick; bottom left: Aero-Pic; bottom right: Judith Gefter
Page 80 - 81: Alexandre Georges
Page 82: Reference desk photo: Alexandre Georges; all others: Taylor Hardwick
Page 83: Bottom left: Taylor Hardwick; all others: Alexandre Georges
Page 84: Alexandre Georges
Page 85: Renderings: Taylor Hardwick; bottom left: Aero-Pic; all others: Alexandre Georges
Page 86: photo of 1905 Jacksonville Public Library: Taylor Hardwick
Page 88: Robin Clark
Page 89: Wade Sweicord
Page 90: Rendering: Taylor Hardwick; all others: Wade Sweicord
Page 91: Top left: Wade Sweicord; top right: Laura Alexander
Page 92: Wade Sweicord
Page 93: Top photo: Alexandre Georges; rendering by Robert Broward
Page 95: Taylor Hardwick
Page 96: 1.: Larry Coldwell; 2.: Edgar Cardell; 3.: Anita Hardwick; 4. & 5. Taylor Hardwick
Page 97: 7., 8., 9., 10.:Taylor Hardwick; 11.: Gay Hardwick
Pages 98 - 106: Taylor Hardwick
Page 107: Top left and top right: Michael Dunlap; bottom left: Blue Dog Aerial Photography; bottom right: Jo Hardwick
Page 110: Michael Dunlap

Index

1661 Medical Building 9, 50
1961 Ford Thunderbird 95, 96

Acosta Bridge 59, 63
A History of the Haydon Burns Library 86
antique frame 99
Architectural Forum 46
Architectural Record 50
Atlantic Beach 1, 14, 56
Atrium, Inc. 3, 46, 57, 111
The Auchter Company 87
Avondale 27

Baymeadows Super Pool 107
Beakes, O.C. Residence 28
Broward, Robert 93
Brown, George Residence 40

Carnegie Foundation 86
Cemesto 10, 16
The Chapel Oak 68
Cinder 96
Cinderbird 95, 96
Citizens Committee for Progress and Park Improvement Referendum 77
City of Jacksonville 23, 63, 78, 86, 87, 88, 108
Clifton 11, 19
Commercial Projects
 1661 Medical Building 9
 Atrium, Inc. 57
 The Credit Bureau of Jacksonville 54
 Fletcher Building 59
 Good, Dr. Harry, Orthodontist, Office Building of 60
 The Group Gallery 57
 Hardwick & Lee Offices 46
 Harry James Insurance Office 48
 Harvey, W. M. Office Building 65
 Holmberg Construction Company Office 62
 Hughes Brothers Filling Station 58
 Mathews, Osborne & Ehrlich Law Offices 55
 McKay, Dr. Charles Office Building 49
 McKesson & Robbins Office and Warehouse 55
 Murray Hill Barnett Bank 49
 National Auto Insurance Company 56
 Nitram Chemicals Office Building 64
 Skinner Dairy Stores 52
 Someplace Else 63
 United Electric Company 53
corn crib 14, 96
Costa Rica 89
The Credit Bureau of Jacksonville 54

Dallas Graham Library 87
Dansk 57
Daughtery, Edward 78
Davidson, Michael Residence 35
Diamondhead Restaurant 63
Discotheque 63
Doctors Lake 38, 39, 68
Drake, Kenyon 1, 2, 109
Dunlap, Michael iii, 109
Dunlap, Rex 47, 57
Duval County Public Schools 73
Duval County Schools 75
Dux 57

Eames, Charles 55
Empire Point 16

First Christian Church of Jacksonville 1
Five Points 9, 59

Flat Top 10
Fleming, Jr., Francis P. 93
Fletcher Building 4, 59, 105
Fletcher, Jerome and Paul 63
Fletcher, John Z. 59
Florence Pitti Palace 13
Florida Machine & Foundry Company 16
Florida Physicians Insurance Company 4
Florida School for the Deaf and Blind 70
Frank, Pat 10
Friendship Park 4, 63, 77

Gainesville, Florida 89
Gardner, Asa 77
Gatsby's 63
Georges, Alexandre 109
Girard, Alexander 57
Good, Dr. Harry, Orthodontist, Office Building of 60
The Green Derby 2, 3
Greene, Milton H. 111
Gregg, Jennifer Johnson Residence 27
The Group Gallery 3, 57

Hall, William 57
Hardwick, Charles 57
Hardwick, Jo iii
Hardwick & Lee iii, 7, 11, 18, 45, 46, 48, 49, 53, 55, 57, 58, 59, 67, 68, 70, 71, 73, 78, 87, 89, 102, 103, 104, 106, 109
Hardwick & Lee Offices 46
Hardwick, Margie 109
Hardwick, Taylor i, iii, 1, 2, 3, 4, 7, 8, 9, 13, 14, 23, 45, 46, 48, 52, 57, 67, 72, 78, 80, 84, 87, 88, 93, 95, 97, 108, 109, 110, 111
Hardwick, Taylor Residence, Atlantic Beach 14
Hardwick, Taylor Residence, Bayview 8
Hardwick, Taylor Residence, Ortega 23
Harry James Insurance Office 48
Harvey, Bill 9
Harvey, W. M. Office Building 65
Haydon Burns Library i, 4, 26, 67, 84, 86, 88, 105
Haydon Burns Public Library i, 80, 87
Heinrich, Dr. Edwin P. 68
Henry John Klutho Award 87
Herman Miller 57
Holmberg Construction Company Office 62
Holmberg, Phillip Residence 34
Holmes, Jacqueline 3, 57
Holmes Lumber Company 104
Holmes, Rogers Residence 38
Homosassa Springs 1, 2
Honor Award for Design 60
House and Home Magazine 46
Hughes Brothers Filling Station 58
Hughes Brothers Tire Company 58

Institutional Projects
 Florida School for the Deaf and Blind 70
 Friendship Park and Fountain 77
 Haydon Burns Public Library 80
 Jacksonville Art Museum 93
 J.E.B. Stuart High School 71
 Jefferson Davis High School 73
 Little Hall 89
 St. Johns Country Day School 68
 Wolfson High School 75
Italia Glass 57

Jacksonville Art Museum 93, 104
Jacksonville Beach 10, 49
Jacksonville Chapter of the American Institute of Architects 87
Jacobs, Robert Residence 20

J.E.B. Stuart High School 67, 71
Jefferson Davis High School 73
John Hall Jacobs 86

Kafka Residence 26
King, Marion Residence 11
Klutho Award 87, 108
Klutho, H.J. 80, 86
Knoll 57
Koger, Mrs. Ira 93
Kraus, Gomer 58, 67, 89, 106, 109

Ladies Home Journal 24
l'architecture d'aujourd'Hui 50
Lee, Mayberry 2, 3, 4, 45, 67, 72, 109
Leuthold, Duane 67, 109
Lightolier 57
Little Hall 89, 91
Little, Winston W. 89
Lux, Jonathan 52, 109
Lynch Building 55

Madison, Thomas Jacksonville Residence 32
Madison, Thomas Summer Residence 41
Mandarin 34, 36
Marsh Landing 40
Mathews, Jr. John E. Residence 36
Mathews, Osborne & Ehrlich Law Offices 55
Mayport 20
McCall, Frank 9
McKay, Dr. Charles Office Building 49
McKesson & Robbins Office and Warehouse 55
Metropolitan 57
MG Midget 96
Mid-Century architect iii
Mid-Century Modern i, 4
Morris, Dr. Kenneth 1
motor-scooter 96
Murray Hill 49, 53, 111
Murray Hill Barnett Bank 49
Museum of Contemporary Art Jacksonville 93

Nathan Bedford Forrest High School 76
National Auto Insurance Company 56
Newton, Russell Residence 30
Nitram Chemicals Office Building 64

O'Donoghue Residence 18
Orange Park 22, 30, 38, 68
Ortega 9, 12, 23, 24, 32, 35, 106
Ortega Forest 9

Peacock, Thomas Residence 16
Pedrick Motor Company 95
Pochote tree 89, 91
Ponte Vedra 107
Pottsburg Creek 93
Prober 57

Rada, Rudi 111
Register & Cummings 78, 81
Remington Rand 83
Residential Projects
 Beakes, O.C. Residence 28
 Brown, George Residence 40
 Davidson, Michael Residence 35
 Gregg, Jennifer Johnson Residence 27
 Hardwick, Taylor Residence 23
 Hardwick, Taylor Residence, Atlantic Beach 14
 Hardwick, Taylor Residence, Bayview 8
 Hardwick, Taylor Residence, Ortega 23
 Holmberg, Phillip Residence 34

Holmes, Rogers Residence 38
Jacobs, Robert Residence 20
Kafka Residence 26
King, Marion Residence 11
Madison, Thomas Jacksonville Residence 32
Madison, Thomas Summer Residence 41
Mathews, Jr. John E. Residence 36
Newton, Russell Residence 30
O'Donoghue Residence 18
Peacock, Thomas Residence 16
Soles, John Residence 29
Springfield, Adair Residence 19
Stockton, Waldo Residence 10
Taylor, Champ Residence 9
Varn, George Residence 12
Whitehead Residence 22
Richards Morgenthau 57
Riley, Clayton 3
Riverside 2, 3, 46, 48, 50, 57, 59, 93, 106
Ropp, John 3, 46, 57
Russell, Louise 1

Saarinen, Eero i, 4
Samuel Huckle Award 13
San Jose 18
Seminole Beach 20
Sherman, Frank 77, 78
simplicity 7, 13, 26, 28, 35, 53, 70
Skinner Dairy Stores 52
Soles, John Residence 29
Someplace Else 63
Southbank 63
Southside Businessmen's Club 77
Splinterville 8, 9
Springfield, Adair Residence 19
Squiggle Ceiling 82
State of Florida 70
St. Augustine, Florida 70
St. Johns Country Day School 68
St. John's Episcopal Cathedral 54
St. Johns River 11, 12, 16, 17, 22, 23, 26, 27, 30, 32, 36, 59, 63, 77, 78
Stockton, Waldo Residence 10
Studio M 93

Tampa 64
Taylor, Champ Residence 9
Taylor, Dr. Champ 9, 106
Town & Country 20

United Electric Company 53
University of Florida iii, 4, 89
University of Pennsylvania 1, 13

Varn, George Residence 12
Venetia 26, 28

Wallace, Marvel and Howie 11
Waynesville, North Carolina 41
Welcome to the World 99
Westside 73
Whitehead Residence 22
William E. Arnold Company 78
Williams, Ann 81, 82, 85, 86, 97
Windle Hotel 86
W. Kenyon Drake and Associates 1
Wolfson High School 75, 76
Wood, Wayne i, 84